Origami Sailboats

Also by Lew Rozelle

Origami in King Arthur's Court
Origami Rockets
Origami Ornaments

Origami Sailboats

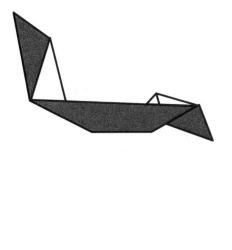

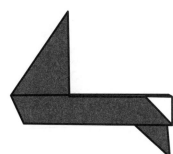

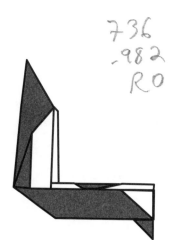

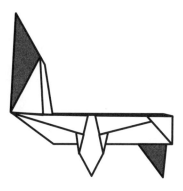

St. Martin's Griffin
New York

**By
Lew Rozelle**

www.stmartins.com

Design: Lew Rozelle
Associate Editor: Dorsey Mills
Production Editor: David Stanford Burr
Copyeditor: Sam Randlett
Proofreader: Gay Merrill Gross

Library of Congress Cataloging-in-Publication Data

Rozelle, Lew.
  Origami sailboats / by Lew Rozelle.— 1st ed.
    p. cm.
  ISBN 0-312-26906-4
    1. Origami. 2. Sailboats. I. Title.

TT870 .R683 2000

736'.982—dc21

200108570

First Edition: February 2002

10 9 8 7 6 5 4 3 2 1

Contents

Sailboat Rudders

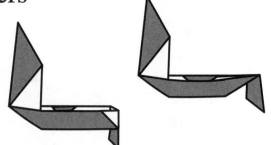

Sailboat Bows and Sterns

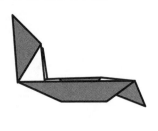

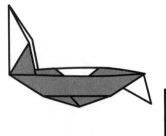

Narrow and Wide Sailboats

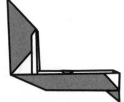

Sailboat Stabilizers

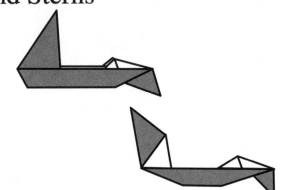

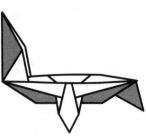

Sailboat Design

Sailing Origami Sailboats

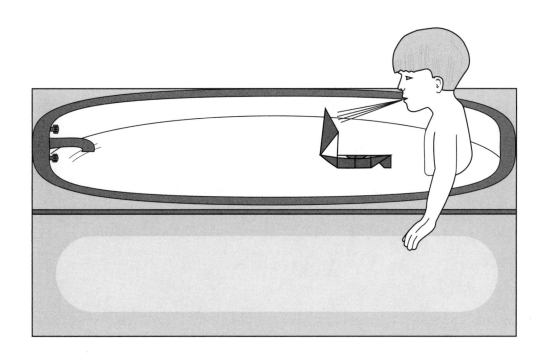

Introduction

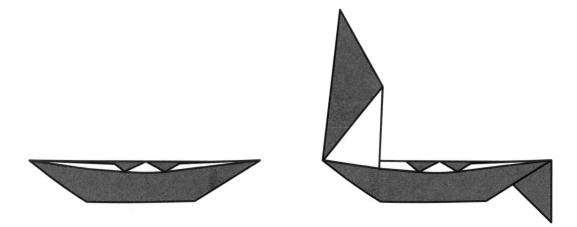

Origami Sailboats developed from a traditional model; the instructions for folding the *inside out boat* have appeared in many origami books over the years. This boat is unusual in that it is turned inside out after it is folded. There are several variations, but they all require that the model be turned inside out, and the utmost care must be taken not to tear the paper. Although the boats float very well, they lack the capacity to trap the wind and move on their own.

Sailboats need a hull, sail, and rudder to move through the water powered by the wind. By modifying the traditional model we can produce a sailboat that meets all these requirements without turning the model inside out.

Origami Sailboats will lead you through the necessary folds, and will, ultimately, allow you to design and fold your own sailboats. I have arranged the models to show how the sailboats were developed: first you fold the traditional boat, then fold the same boat without turning the model inside out. All of these new sailboats require folding a sequence I call the Boat Fold; several simple boats at the beginning of this book serve to introduce this procedure. Once you have mastered the Boat Fold you can begin creating sailboats that will sail with the wind.

Paper boats will last in water for several hours before they begin to lose their shape. If you fold the sailboats from plastic-coated freezer wrap they will last for several days. Freezer-paper and wax-paper sailboats can be removed from the water and allowed to dry; they can then be sailed again.

I hope that you enjoy folding and sailing these *Origami Sailboats* as much as I have.

Lew Rozelle

Learning the Folds

Work through the models in order from beginning to end.

International symbols for folding paper

Valley Fold

Mountain Fold

Fold in Front

Fold Behind

Turn Model Over

Fold and Unfold

Sink or Push In

Watch this Spot

X   Watch this Spot

O   Hold Here

Hold Here and Pull

Symbols

The symbols used in origami are shown at the left. They are the international language of the origami world.

A series of dashes represents a valley fold. Make a concave crease where this line appears.

A series of dots and dashes represents a mountain fold. Make a convex crease wherever this line appears.

Arrows show the directions in which you make the fold: left, right, up, down, in front, behind, and into. These directions refer to the page itself. "Fold upward" means fold toward the top of the page. "Near" is closest to you. "Far" or "behind" is away from you.

Following Directions

First, read the written instructions. "Valley-fold" tells you to make a valley fold. "Repeat steps 3 through 5" gives you instructions which would be difficult to convey in a drawing.

Second, look at the accompanying drawing. The drawing will show you how the model should look as each step in the folding sequence takes place. The arrows will also help you see where to make a fold.

Third, always look ahead to the next drawing to see how the model should look after a fold is made. This will also show you when you have made a mistake. You should go on folding only after you have completed the step successfully.

Procedures

There are several combinations of folds, which when combined produce a desired effect. "Reverse-fold" is a procedure which has several folding steps. These will be explained in the next few pages, before you begin folding. Remember to make each fold as precise as you can. Work through the models **in order** from beginning to end.

Basic Folding

Valley Fold

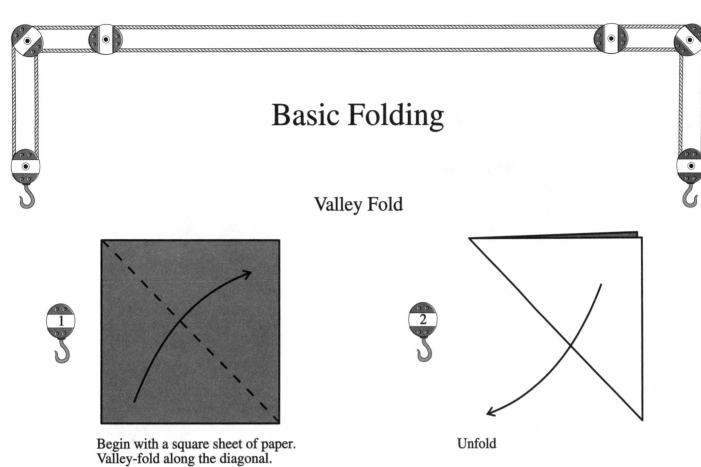

Begin with a square sheet of paper.
Valley-fold along the diagonal.

Unfold

Each of the drawings in this book is part of a folding sequence. Each drawing is accompanied by a small boat-hook containing its number. Carefully follow each step in turn until you have completed a model. The drawing at the left shows a simple valley fold. Notice that the square is shaded: this indicates that the colored side of the paper is facing you. The dashed line shows where the fold takes place. The paper is folded in front creating a valley. Try to be as precise as you can so that the edges of the paper are aligned with each other while the crease is formed.

Mountain Fold

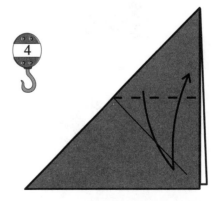

Begin with a square sheet of paper.
Mountain-fold along the diagonal.

Valley-fold the top point down to
the lower right corner and unfold.

The mountain fold is indicated by a different type of line and arrow. The paper is folded behind. (The drawings do not always show the result with photographic accuracy. This freedom in drawing allows you to see where the paper has gone after the fold. In reality you would not be able to see the back edges of the paper in step 4.) Step 3 tells you to mountain-fold the paper and shows where to make the crease. Step 4 tells you to make a valley fold and to unfold it. The double arrow shows that you are to fold and unfold.

Reverse Fold

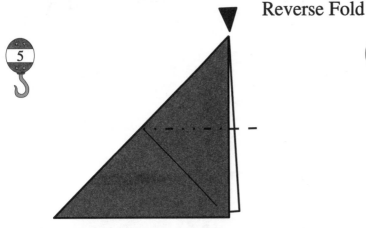

Reverse-fold the top corner of the paper.

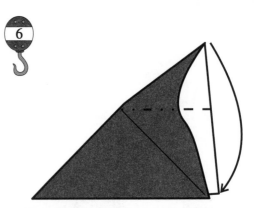

Step 6 shows the reverse fold in progress.

Step 5 shows where to make a mountain fold on the near layer and a valley fold on the far layer. This will allow you to reverse-fold the right corner. The black triangle indicates a reverse fold, so called because the diagonal folded edge—the spine, so to speak—reverses itself, changing from convex to concave. You are going to open up the corner and push the upper corner down into the model, between the front and back layers. Step 6 shows this procedure in progress.

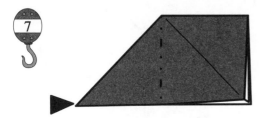

Repeat step 5 on the left corner.

Both reverse folds are now completed.

Step 7 shows the completion of step 6, and tells you to repeat this process on the left corner.

Rabbit Ear

Valley-fold the near flap diagonally in half and unfold.

Valley-fold the near bottom edge up to the crease made in step 9.

Valley-fold the right edge of the near flap to the diagonal crease formed in step 9.

Pull out the flap hidden between the two near layers.

Steps 9 through 13 explain how to make a rabbit ear. Step 9 tells you to valley-fold the near right corner to the upper left point and then unfold. This will leave a crease. Step 10 tells you to fold the near bottom edge of the paper up to the crease formed in step 9. Simply align the edge with the crease and press flat. Step 11 tells you to fold the right edge of the near flap to the diagonal crease line. Step 12 tells you to pull out the tiny flap hidden behind the nearest layer of paper. Do not unfold steps 10–11. The flap is reversed outward from within the construction.

The completed rabbit ear.

Rabbit-ear the near flap as shown.

Step 13 shows the completed folds. Step 14 tells you to form a rabbit ear on the near flap. This is how steps 10 through 12 will appear in the book.

Squash Fold

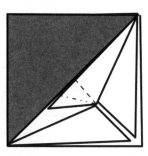

Enlarged view of step 13. Mountain- and valley-fold the tiny flap as shown.

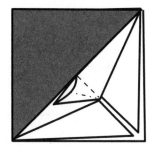

The squash fold is shown here in progress.

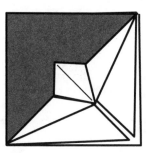

The completed squash fold.

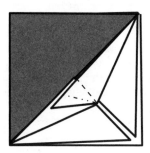

Squash-fold the tiny flap as shown.

Steps 15 through 18 illustrate a squash fold. Step 15 tells where to make a valley and mountain fold. In step 16 simply lift up the center flap and open it. Press down on the flap and (squash) the flap flat. Step 18 shows how the squash fold is illustrated in one step.

Boat Fold

 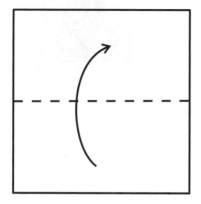

Begin with a square sheet of paper. Valley-fold upward in half.

 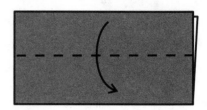

Valley-fold only the near layer in half, downward.

 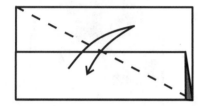

Valley-fold diagonally in half and unfold. Don't let the layers slide apart!

Repeat step 3 along the opposite diagonal. Don't let the layers slide apart!

 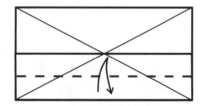

Valley-fold the bottom edges up to the central folded edge and unfold.

 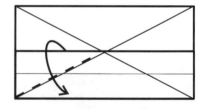

Valley-fold the near left corner down along the crease formed in step 4.

 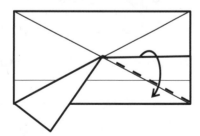

Valley-fold the near right corner down along the crease formed in step 3.

 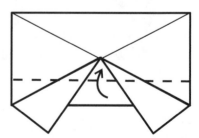

Valley-fold the lower portion of the model up along the crease formed in step 5.

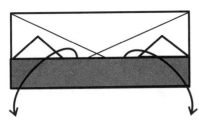

Unfold completely.

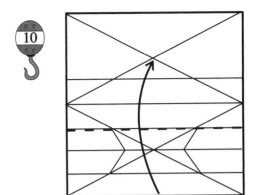

Valley-fold upward the three lowest horizontal segments.

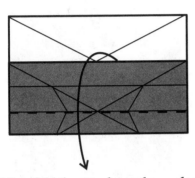

Valley-fold the near layer down along the indicated existing crease.

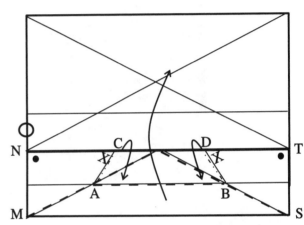

Enlarged View. Pull point C clockwise downward. Corner M will begin to rise along the diagonal crease formed in step 4. As M rises toward N and the model is flattened, mountain fold AC will form itself. Repeat on the right, pulling point D counterclockwise. Watch the spots marked X. Watch the black dots.

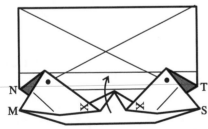

Step 13 shows these folds in progress. Swing the bottom upward and flatten the model to begin formation of the hull.

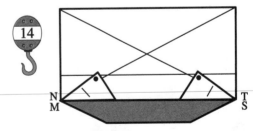

The moutain and valley folds in step 12 make up the Boat Fold.

Steps 1 through 11 form creases that prepare a Boat Fold. Step 12 shows the Boat Fold notation. The configuration remains exactly the same for all the boats. The following two boats will allow you to practice this fold.

Traditional Boat

(Traditional Fold)

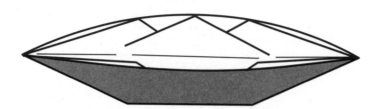

 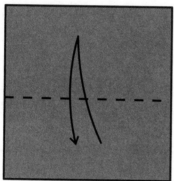

Begin by valley-folding a square in half.
Unfold.

 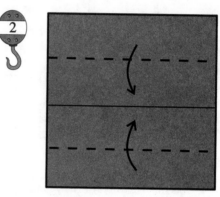

Valley-fold the top and bottom edges to the
centerline.

 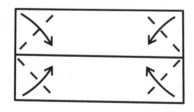

Valley-fold all four corners to the centerline.

 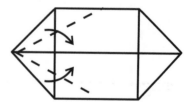

Valley-fold the top and bottom left corners to the
centerline.

 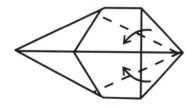

Repeat step 4 on the top and bottom right corners.

 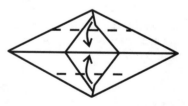

Valley-fold the top and bottom points to the
centerline.

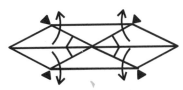

Open the central horizontal raw edges and turn the model inside out; after you open the central slit, push at the black arrowheads to invert the corners. Look ahead to steps 8 and 9, and be careful not to tear the paper.

 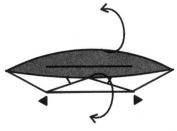 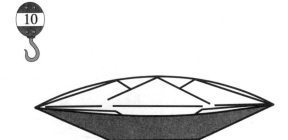

Steps 8 and 9 show this procedure in progress. Rotate the model to the position shown in step 9.

 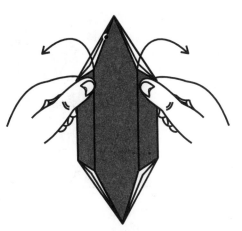

The completed Traditional Boat.

Place your thumbs on the inside edges and hold your index fingers on the corners at the back; gently press the corners toward yourself until they pop into a shape that is convex from your point of view. Repeat this process on the lower half to turn the model completely inside out. Don't worry if the bow and stern tend to tear on your first few attempts! You may want to try the tough paper of a brown grocery bag.

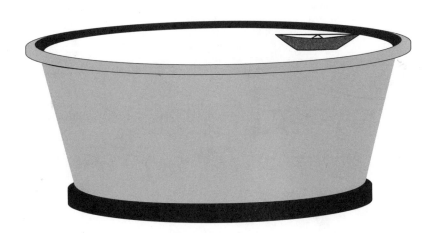

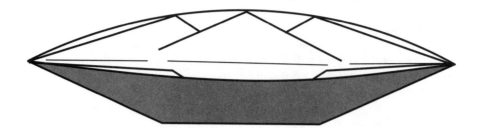

Double-Ended Boat

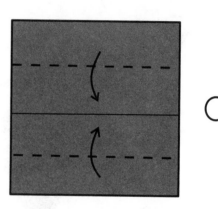

1

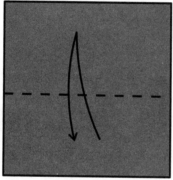

Begin this second boat by folding a square in half. Unfold.

2

Valley-fold the top and bottom edges to the center and **turn the model over.**

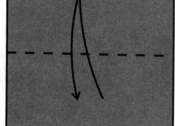
3

Valley-fold the top and bottom edges to the center.

4

Swing the raw edges out from behind.

5

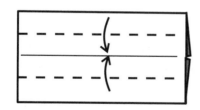

Valley-fold the model in half along both diagonals and unfold.

6

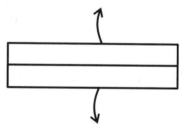

N • • T

M S

Mountain- and valley-fold the bottom half of the model using the Boat Fold configuration. Watch the black dots.

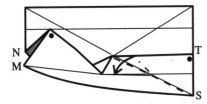 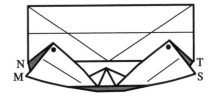

Step 7 shows the Boat Fold in progress.
Watch the black dots.

Flatten the boat.

  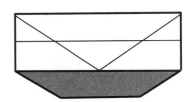

Valley-fold the triangular flaps in half and then
valley-fold them again, tucking them down
into the hull of the boat.

Repeat steps 6 through 9 on the top half of the
model.

 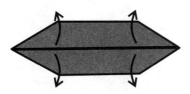 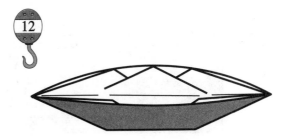

Open the sides of the boat. Do not turn
the model inside out.

The simple Double-Ended Boat will float.
We have duplicated the structure of the
Traditional Boat without the inside-out
procedure.

Boat

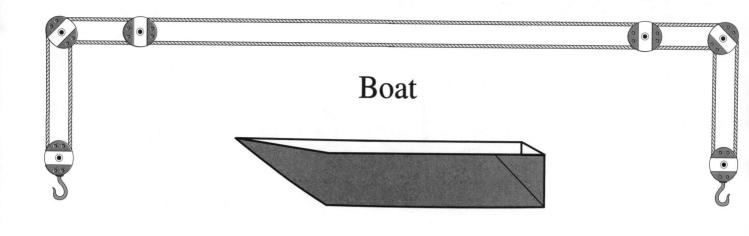

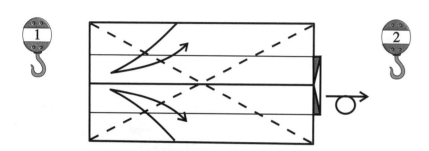

1 Begin with a step 5 of the Double-Ended Boat (page 10). Valley-fold and unfold the diagonals. **Turn the model over.**

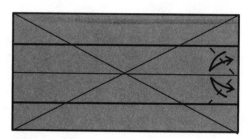

2 Valley-fold the near right corners to the centerline and unfold.

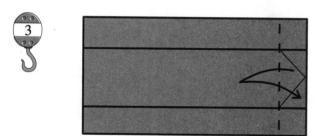

3 Valley-fold the right end of the model as shown. Unfold.

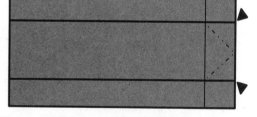

4 Reverse-fold the two triangular flaps into the model along the creases formed in step 2.

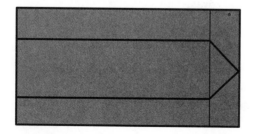

5 **Turn the model over** from top to bottom.

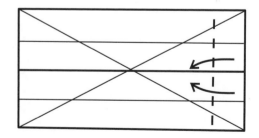

6 Valley-fold the near right layers leftward along the crease formed in step 3.

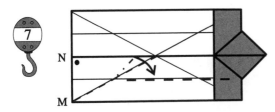

Boat-fold the bottom left side by mountain- and valley-folding the near layers as shown. Watch the black dot.

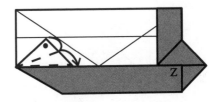

Step 8 shows this fold in progress. Watch the black dot.

 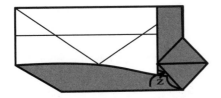

Continue until the bottom raw edge aligns with the horizontal centerline, and then flatten the model. Watch the black dot.

 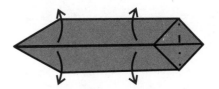

Valley-fold the inner triangular flap down to the raw edge, and then fold it again, tucking it down into the hull. Note corner Z.

 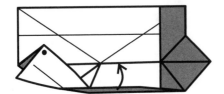

Tuck corner Z into the pocket behind it. Repeat steps 7 through 11 on the top half of the boat.

Open the sides of the boat without turning the model inside out. Square the stern by pinching its corners into the mountain folds indicated.

 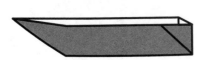

The simple Boat has a flat stern called a transom.

Sailboat Base

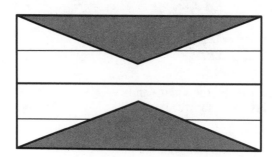

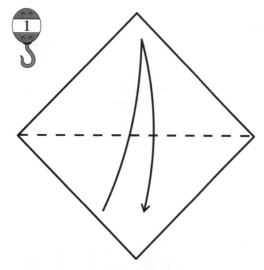

Begin to accordion-fold the paper by valley-folding along the diagonal; unfold.

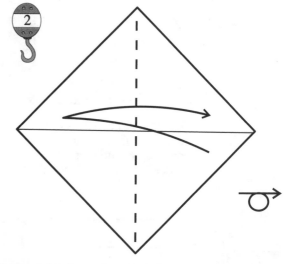

Valley-fold along the other diagonal and unfold. **Turn over**.

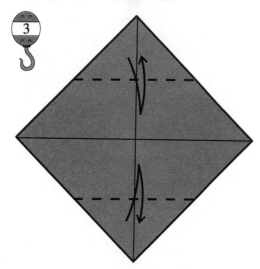

Valley-fold the top and bottom points to the center and unfold.

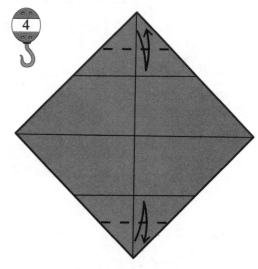

Valley-fold the top and bottom points to the crease made in step 3 and unfold.

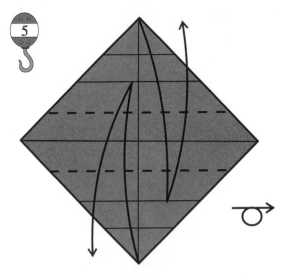

Valley-fold the top and bottom corners over the centerline to the crease formed in step 3 and unfold. **Turn the model over**.

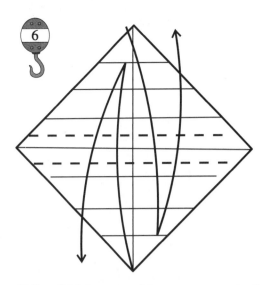

Valley-fold the top and bottom corners to the crease formed in step 4 and unfold.

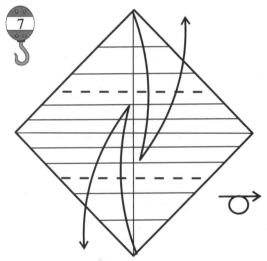

Valley-fold the top and bottom corners to the crease formed in step 5 and unfold. **Turn the model over**.

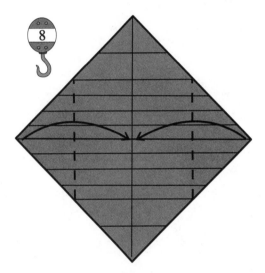

Valley-fold the side corners to the center.

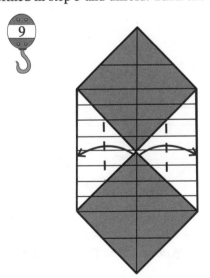

Valley-fold the inside corners to the outer edges.

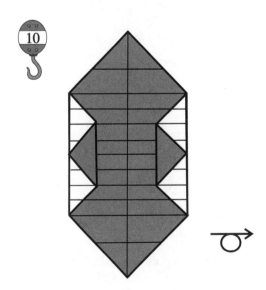

Turn the model over.

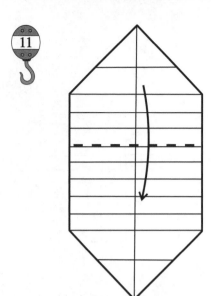

Valley-fold the top point down along the crease formed in step 6.

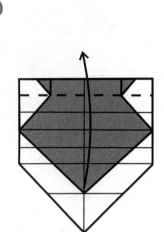

Valley-fold the near point up along the crease formed in step 5.

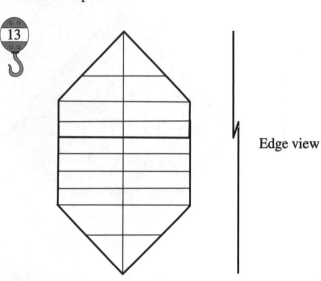

Edge view

Repeat steps 11 and 12 on the bottom half of the model.

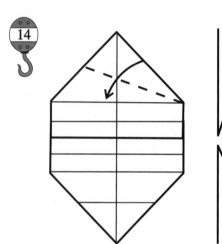

Valley-fold the top right edge down to the crease formed in step 3.

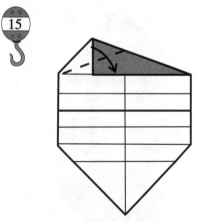

Valley-fold the top left edge down to the crease formed in step 3.

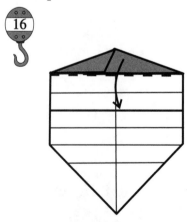

Valley-fold the top down along the crease formed in step 3.

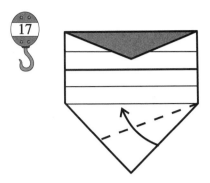

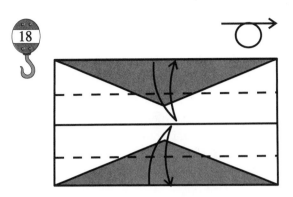

Valley-fold as indicated. Then repeat steps 15 and 16 on the bottom of the model.

Enlarged view. Valley-fold the upper and lower edges to the centerline and unfold. Don't let the layers slide apart! **Turn the Sailboat Base over.**

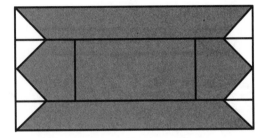

The two nearest pointed colored flaps at left and right will later form the sail and rudder.

The Sailboat Base is a physical structure, a starting point that will be used again and again in this book. The Boat Fold, on the other hand, is a procedure. Make a sample of the Sailboat Base, label it, and keep it with this book for reference. And, looking ahead, fold an extra copy of step 9 on page 22 (the Sailboat Base boat-folded), label it as the Boat Fold, and keep it with the basic Sailboat Base.

Sailboat Part Names

It will help to learn some of the terms used in sailing. Unlike actual sailboats, these origami sailboats have their sails on the bow rather than in the middle or amidship. All of these origami sailboats are flat-bottom boats and will actually sail on any body of water.

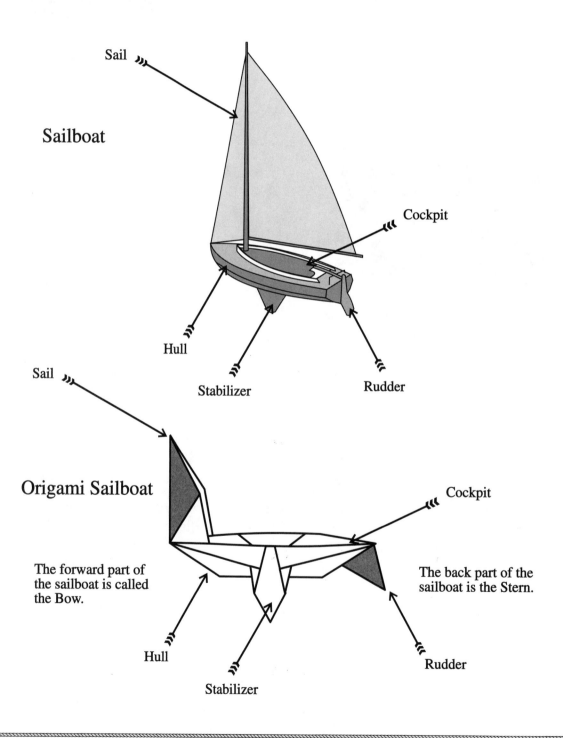

Sail

Sailboat

Cockpit

Hull

Stabilizer

Rudder

Sail

Origami Sailboat

Cockpit

The forward part of the sailboat is called the Bow.

The back part of the sailboat is the Stern.

Hull

Stabilizer

Rudder

Basic Sailboat Parts

How to fold the Hull

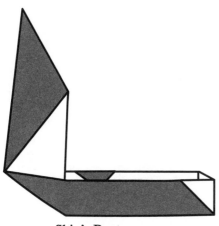

Rowboat

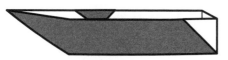

Lifeboat

How to fold the Sail

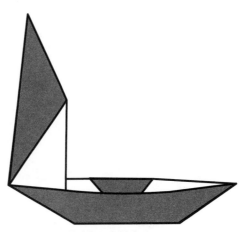

Ship's Boat

Sailing Lifeboat

How to fold the Rudder

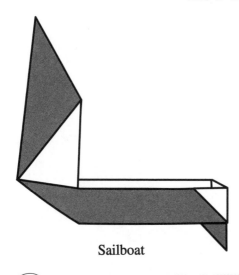

Sailboat

Double-Ended Sailboat

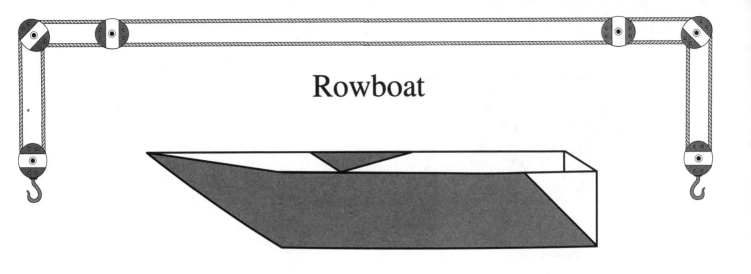

Rowboat

1

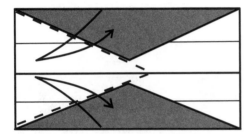

Begin with a Sailboat Base (page 14).
Valley-fold the top and bottom left side of
the model along the folded edges of the
near flaps from the corners all the way to
the centerline and unfold. This begins to
form the bow of the Rowboat. **Turn the
model over** top to bottom .

2

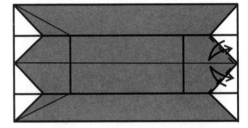

The creases formed in step 1 will still be
on the left. Valley-fold the right near
corners to the centerline and unfold.

3

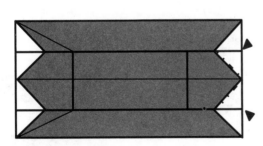

Reverse-fold the near right central
corners into the model.

4

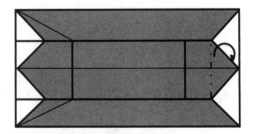

Tuck in the near right flap (a single-layer
triangle). You will have to open the
model slightly to accomplish this.

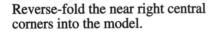

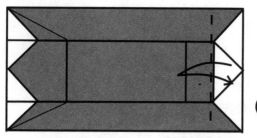

Valley-fold and unfold the right side of the model along the crease formed in step 4. **Turn the model over top to bottom**.

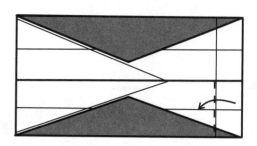

The creases formed in step 1 remain on the left. Valley-fold the bottom right edge leftward along the crease formed in step 5. A triangular collar will form itself.

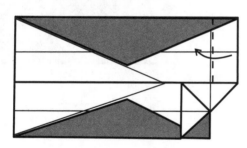

Repeat step 6 at the top.

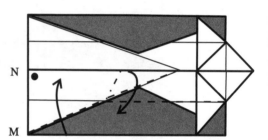

Mountain- and valley-fold the bottom left side into the Boat Fold configuration. The bottom edge will rise to form the side of the boat. Watch the black dot.

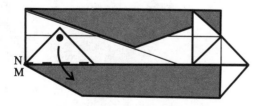

Valley-fold downward the triangular flap formed in step 8.

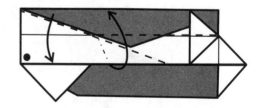

Repeat step 8 on the top half of the model. Watch the black dot.

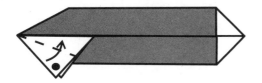

Valley-fold the near flap in half as shown.

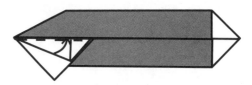

Tuck the newly formed flap up into the model.

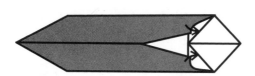

Lift the near flap upward.

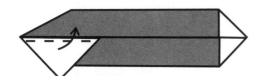

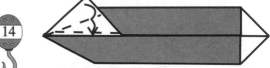

Valley-fold the near flap in half and then tuck it down into the model.

Tuck the inner right corners into the triangular pockets that lie behind them.

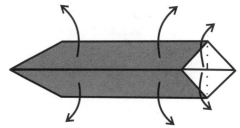

Open out the model and square off the transom.

Side view of the Rowboat.

When you begin to add sails, the sail will be incorporated into the folding of the hull.

Lifeboat

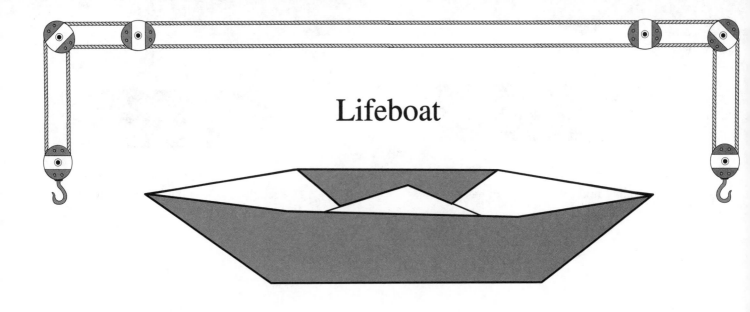

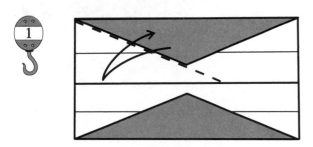

Begin with a Sailboat Base (page 14). Valley-fold all layers diagonally along the folded edge as shown and unfold.

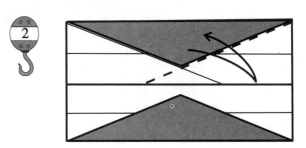

Repeat step 1 at the upper right.

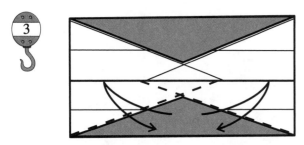

Repeat steps 1 and 2 at the bottom.

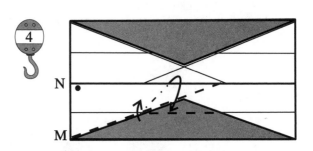

Boat-fold the left portion of the bottom flap. Watch the black dot.

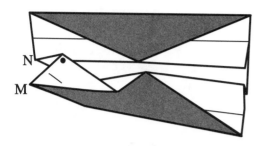

Step 5 shows this procedure in progress.
Watch the black dot.

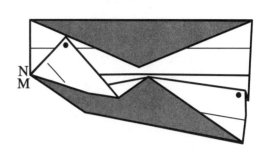

Repeat step 4 on the right bottom half of the
model. Watch the black dot.

Flatten the white inner flaps and bring the near side of
the hull upward around them. Flatten the model.

Valley-fold the near triangular flaps
down over the hull.

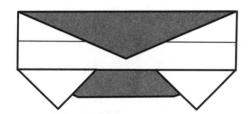

Repeat steps 4 through 7 on the upper
half of the model.

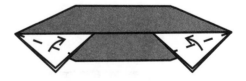

Valley-fold the near flaps in half as
shown.

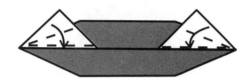

Tuck the newly formed flaps up into the hull.

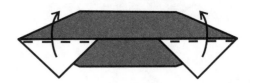

Valley-fold the near flaps upward.

 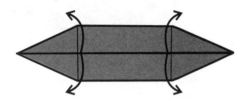

Repeat steps 10 and 11.

Valley-fold and unfold the left and right points as shown.

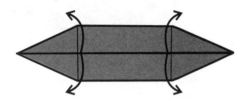

Grasp the edges of the near and inside flaps and open up the lifeboat. Form the hull as shown in steps 16 and 17.

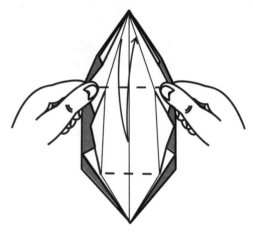

Grasp the sides of the hull and valley-fold the model between the corners and unfold. Repeat at the bottom.

 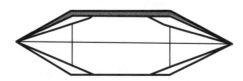

Inside view of the Lifeboat. The innermost flaps are shown flattened onto the hull. Lift them up to lie against the hull. The actions of step 16 allow the boat to remain open.

Side view of the Lifeboat.

Ship's Boat

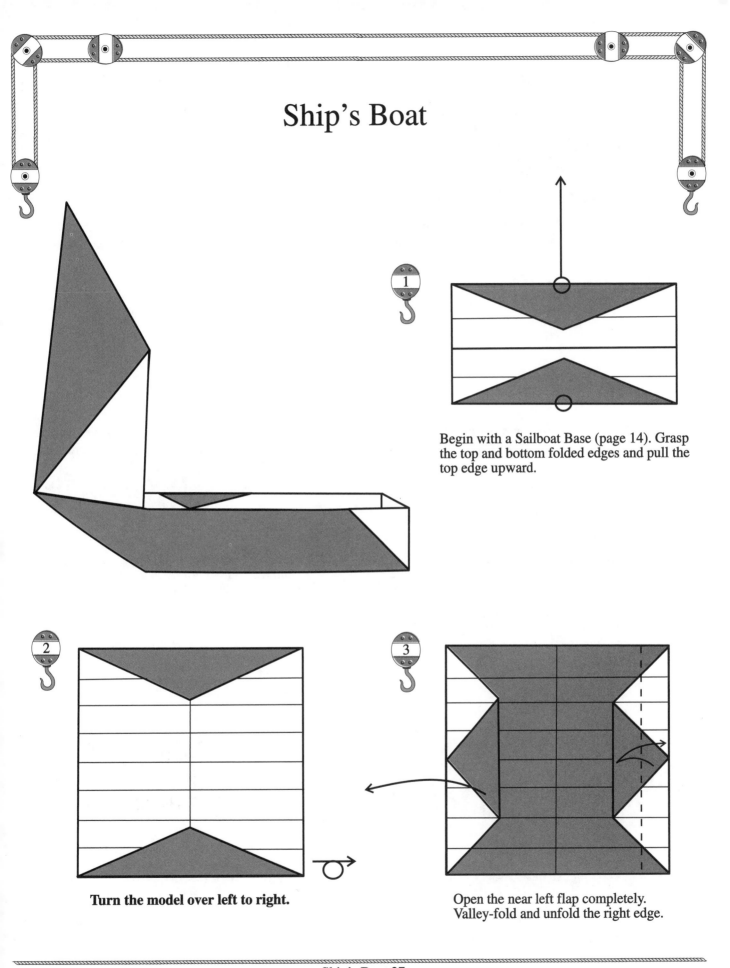

1

Begin with a Sailboat Base (page 14). Grasp the top and bottom folded edges and pull the top edge upward.

2

Turn the model over left to right.

3

Open the near left flap completely. Valley-fold and unfold the right edge.

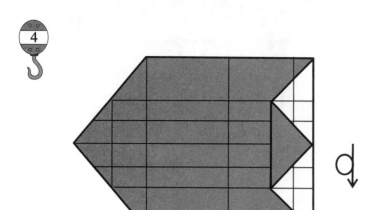

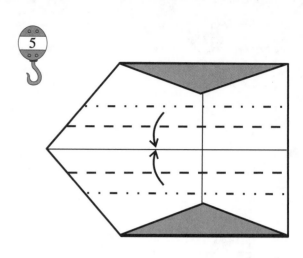

Turn the model over top to bottom.

Refold the horizontal valley and mountain folds so that the model looks like step 6.

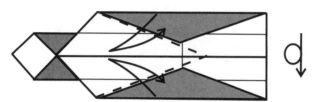

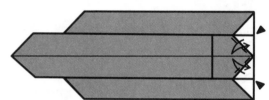

Valley-fold and unfold all layers of the top and bottom left flaps along the near folded edges. This left end will ultimately form the bow of the boat. **Turn the model over.**

Valley-fold the near right central corners to the centerline, and unfold. Then reverse-fold the corners into the model.

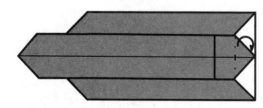

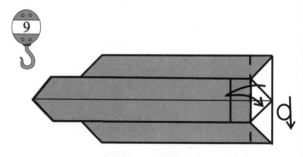

Tuck in the single-layer triangle. You will have to open the model slightly to accomplish this.

Valley-fold and unfold the right side of the model along the edge of the tucked-in flap from step 8. **Turn the model over.**

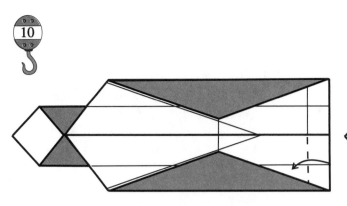

10 Enlarged view. Valley-fold the bottom right edge leftward along the crease formed in step 9. A triangular collar will form itself.

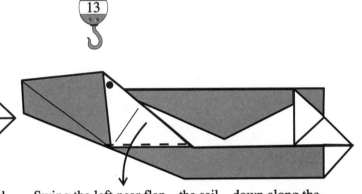

11 Repeat step 10 at the top.

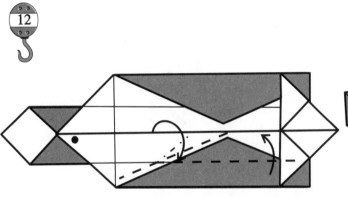

12 Boat-fold the bottom left flap using the same method used for step 8 of the Rowboat (page 21). As you pull the white edge down clockwise and begin to form the near side of the boat, the black-dotted flap will start to rise to form the sail. Flatten the model, and watch the black dot.

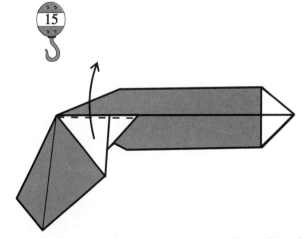

13 Swing the left near flap—the sail—down along the centerline, opening the sail partway. Repeat step 12 on the top. Although the flap is larger than that of the Rowboat, the folding remains the same. Flatten the sail downward.

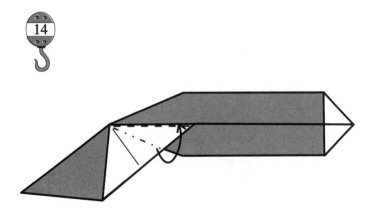

14 Swivel the near portion of the sail up into the model. This will form the near half of the sail.

15 Valley-fold the sail upward and repeat the tucking-in of step 14. Flatten the sail downward.

16

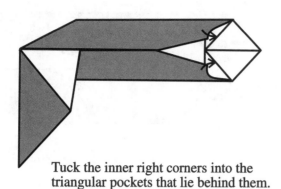

Tuck the inner right corners into the
triangular pockets that lie behind them.

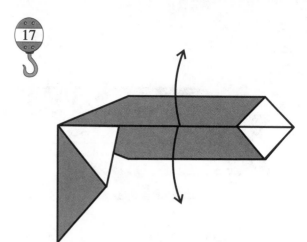

17

Open sides of the boat. Rotate the model
so that the sail points toward the top.

18

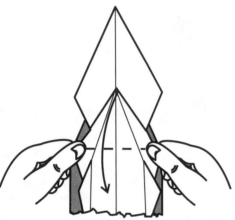

Grasp the sides of the hull and valley-fold its
sail-end downward between the corners. Unfold.
This process will allow the boat to remain open.

19

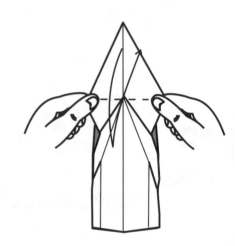

Grasp the sides of the sail, and valley-fold it
downward; then allow the sail to open itself upward
again. Square the transom as in step 16 of the
Rowboat.

20

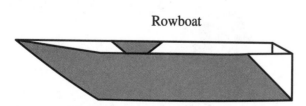

Rowboat

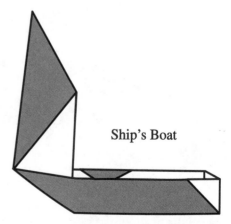

Ship's Boat

The folding of the hull for the Rowboat and the hull for the Ship's Boat remains the same. A simple sail has been
formed by bringing up a large triangular flap. This boat will sail very well but may tend to wander from a
straight course.

Sailing Lifeboat

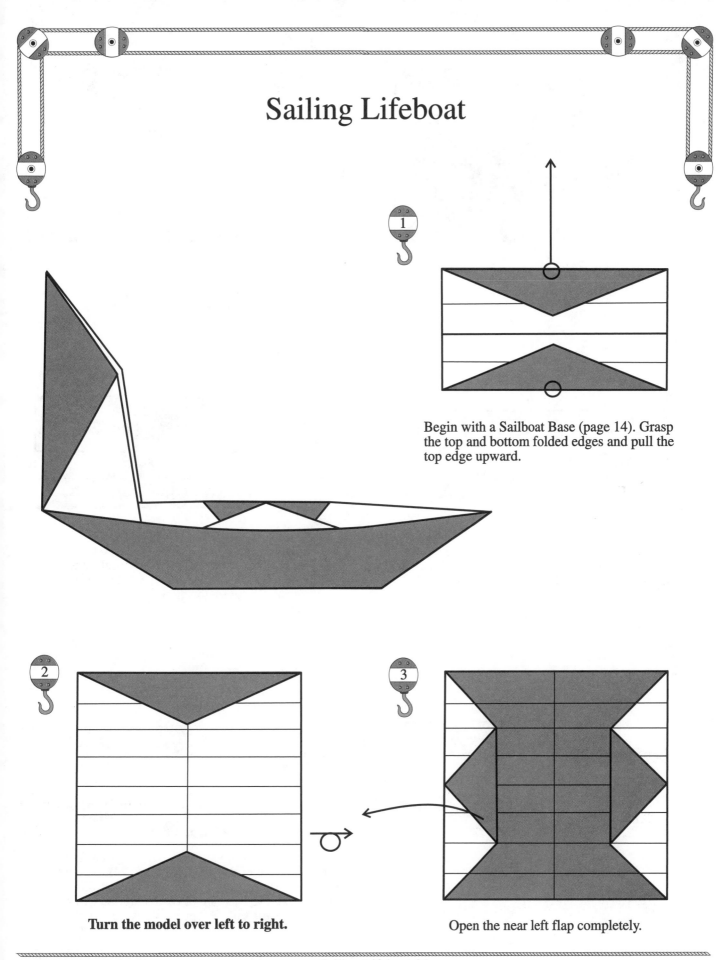

1

Begin with a Sailboat Base (page 14). Grasp the top and bottom folded edges and pull the top edge upward.

2

Turn the model over left to right.

3

Open the near left flap completely.

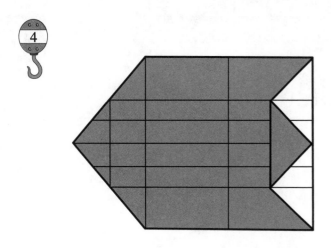

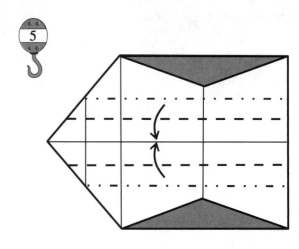

Turn the model over top to bottom.

Refold the horizontal valley and mountain folds so that the model looks like step 6.

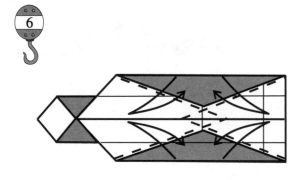

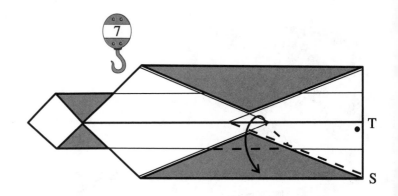

Valley-fold and unfold all the layers of the top and bottom left flaps of the model along the folded edges. Repeat on the right side of the model. These folds begin to form the hull.

Enlarged view. Boat-fold the right portion of the bottom flap down, pulling the central folded edge counterclockwise. Corner S will rise counterclockwise toward point T. Watch the black dot.

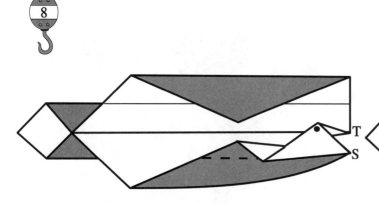

The action of step 7 is shown here in progress. Continue to bring S up toward T. Watch the black dot.

Boat-fold the bottom left flap using the same method used for step 8 of the Rowboat (page 22). As you pull the white edge down clockwise and begin to form the near side of the boat, the black-dotted flap will start to rise to form the sail. Flatten the model, and watch the black dot.

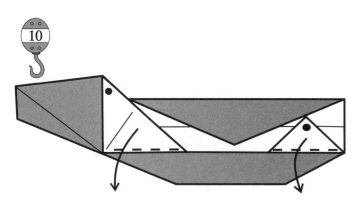

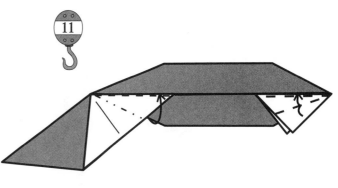

Valley-fold the near left and right flaps downward enough to open the top half of the model. Then repeat steps 7 through 9 on the top half. Although the flap is larger than that of the Lifeboat, the folding remains the same. Flatten the sail downward.

Swivel the near portion of the left flap up into the model. This will form the near half of the sail. Valley-fold the near right flap and tuck it up into the model. Flatten the sail downward.

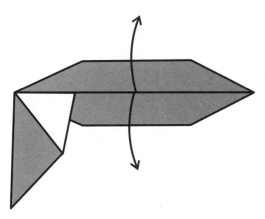

Valley-fold the near left and right flaps upward and repeat the actions of step 11. Flatten the sail downward.

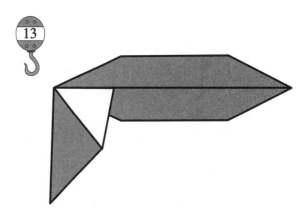

The large flap remaining on the outside of the hull will open to form the sail. The rest of the model remains the same as the Lifeboat.

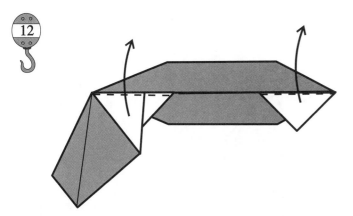

Open out the sides of the hull and bring the sail end to the top.

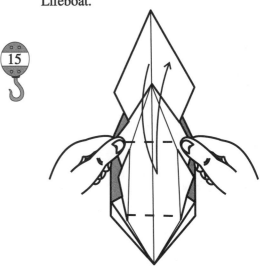

Grasp the sides of the hull and valley-fold between the corners and unfold. Repeat at the bottom.

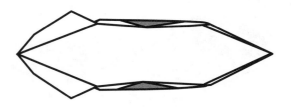

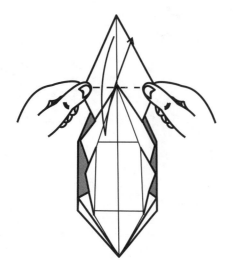

Grasp the sides of the sail and valley-fold it downward; then allow the sail to open itself upward again. This will keep the sail open.

Top view of the Sailing Lifeboat.

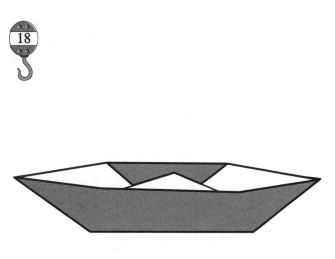

Lifeboat

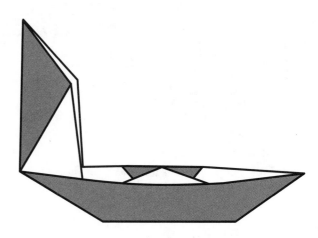

Sailing Lifeboat

The folding of the hull for the Lifeboat and the hull for the Sailing Lifeboat remains the same. A flap from beneath the bow has become the sail.

Sailboat

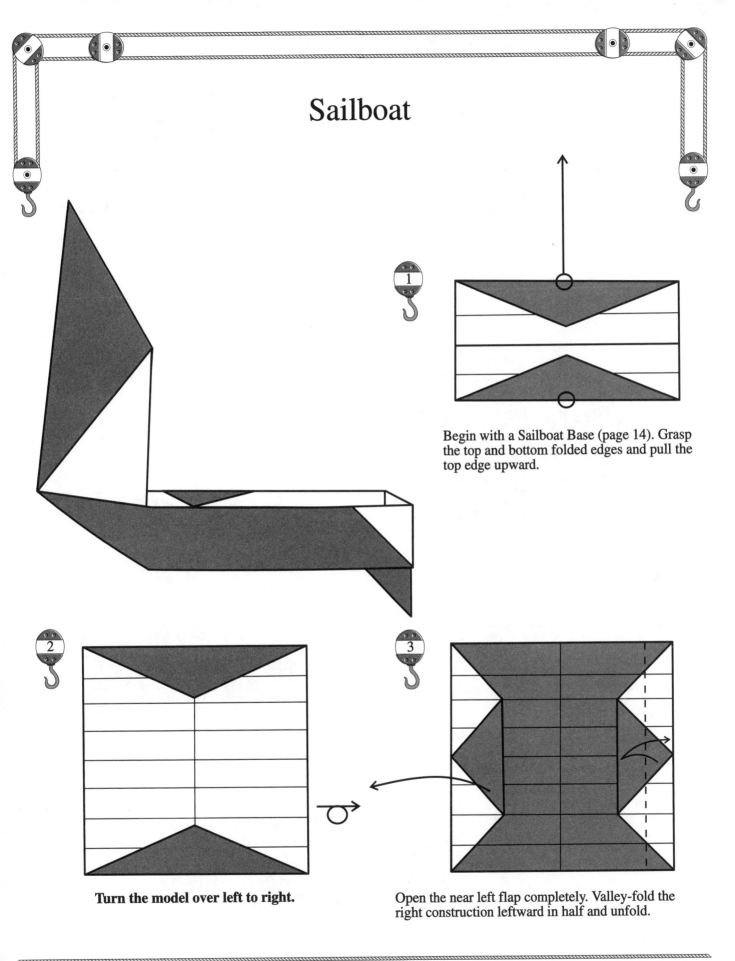

1

Begin with a Sailboat Base (page 14). Grasp the top and bottom folded edges and pull the top edge upward.

2

Turn the model over left to right.

3

Open the near left flap completely. Valley-fold the right construction leftward in half and unfold.

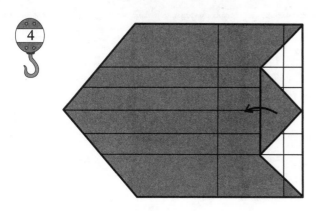

Unfold the near right flap.

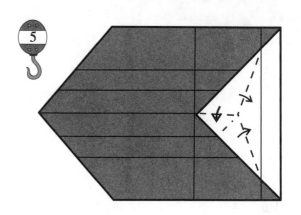

Rabbit-ear the near flap to the crease formed in step 3.

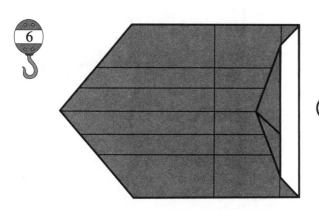

Turn the model over.

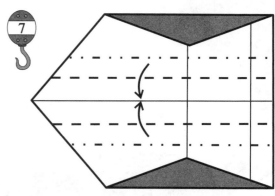

Refold the valley and mountain folds so that the model looks like step 8.

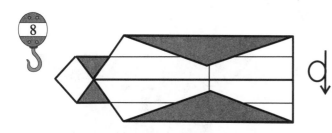

Turn the model over. Many models will begin with step 8 of the Sailboat. Fold an extra copy, label it, and keep it with this book!

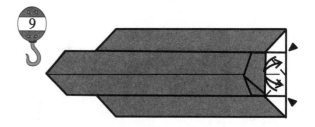

Valley-fold and unfold the right near inner corners to the centerline; then reverse-fold the corners into the model.

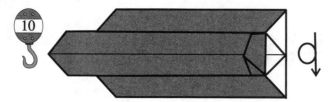

Turn the model over.

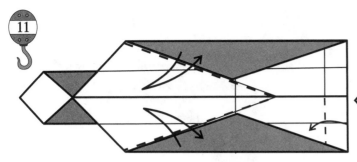

Valley-fold all layers at the left along the folded edges and unfold. Then valley-fold the bottom right edge leftward along the crease formed in step 3. A triangular collar will form itself as the corner is flattened.

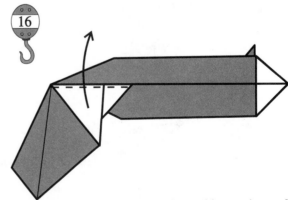

Repeat step 11 on the top right side of the model.

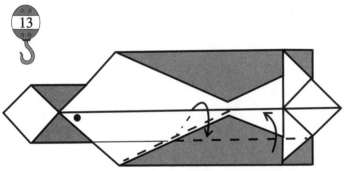

Boat-fold the bottom left flap. As you pull the white edge down clockwise, the black-dotted flap will begin to open into the sail. Watch the black dot.

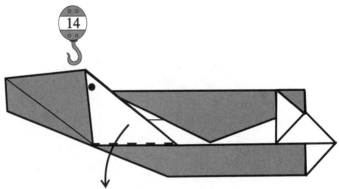

Swing the left near flap down along the centerline, opening the sail partway. Then repeat step 13, boat-folding the top half. Flatten the sail downward.

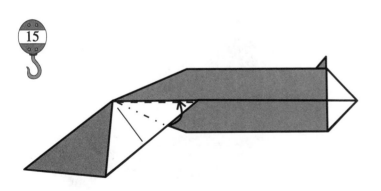

Swivel the near layers of the sail up into the hull. This will form the near half of the sail.

Swing the sail upward. Then repeat the tucking actions of step 15. Flatten the sail downward.

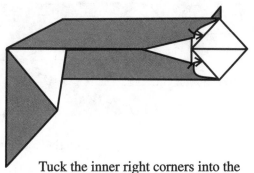

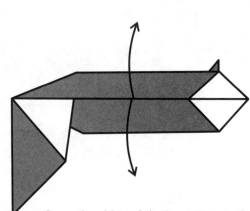

Tuck the inner right corners into the
triangular pockets that lie behind them.

Open the sides of the boat. Rotate the
model so that the sail is toward the top.

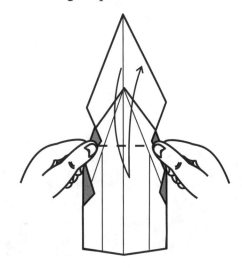

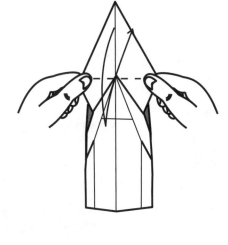

Grasp the sides of the hull and valley-fold the
model downward between the corners and
unfold. Pinch the transom into its square form.

Grasp the sides of the sail; valley-fold
downward and let the sail rise again. Adjust
the rudder to point downward.

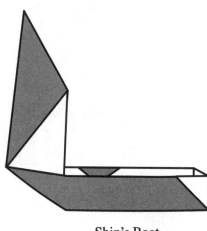

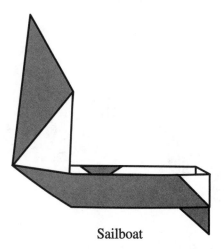

Ship's Boat

Sailboat

The folding of the hull for the Ship's Boat and the hull for the Sailboat remains the same. The rudder will help
the sailboat to remain on a straight course.

Double-Ended Sailboat

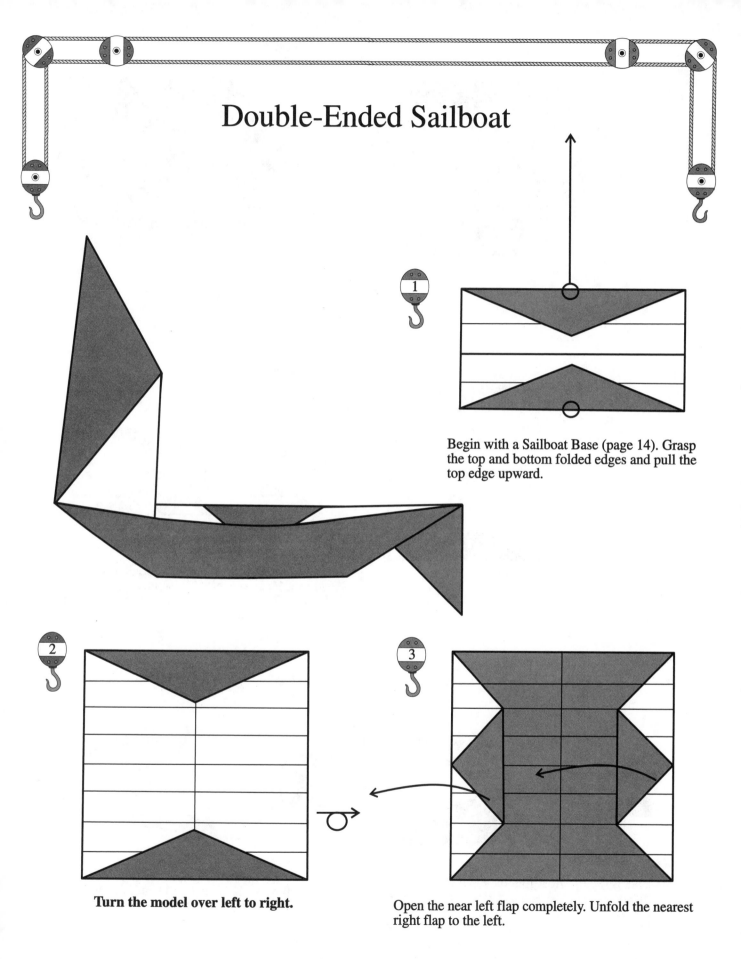

1

Begin with a Sailboat Base (page 14). Grasp the top and bottom folded edges and pull the top edge upward.

2

Turn the model over left to right.

3

Open the near left flap completely. Unfold the nearest right flap to the left.

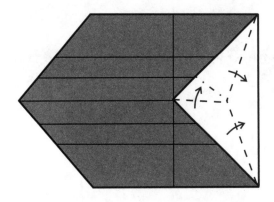

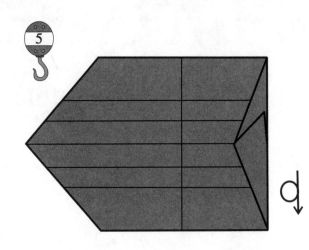

Rabbit-ear the near right flap.

The newly formed flap will become the rudder. **Turn the model over.**

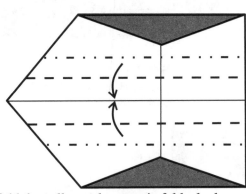

Refold the valley and mountain folds; look ahead to step 7.

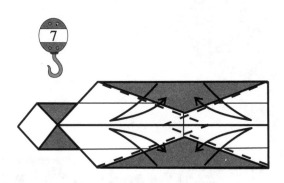

Valley-fold all layers along the folded edges and unfold. Many models will begin with step 7 of the Double-Ended Sailboat. Fold an extra copy, label it, and keep it with this book!

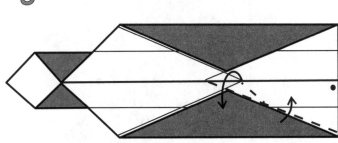

Enlarged view. Boat-fold the the lower right flap by pulling its edge counterclockwise. The dotted corner will rise counterclockwise; watch the black dot.

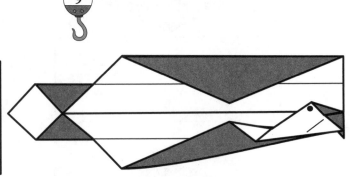

Step 9 shows this procedure in progress. Allow the right end of the hull to rise partway. Watch the black dot.

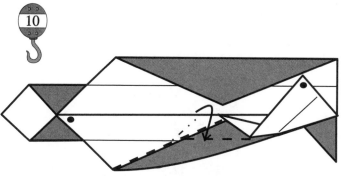

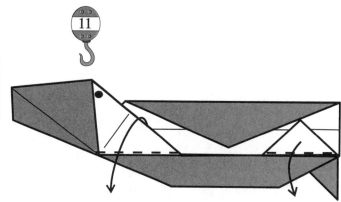

Boat-fold on the left. The large dotted flap will rise clockwise to become the sail. Now flatten the model.

Swing down the near left and right flaps to expose the top half of the model. Repeat steps 8 through 10 on the top half.

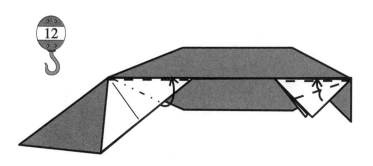

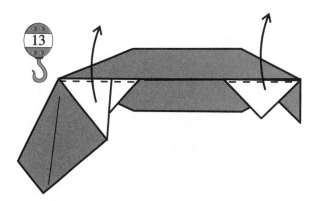

Swivel the near half of the sail up into the model. Valley-fold the near right flap and tuck it into the model. Flatten the sail downward.

Swing the near left and right flaps upward and repeat the actions of step 12 on both flaps. Flatten the sail downward.

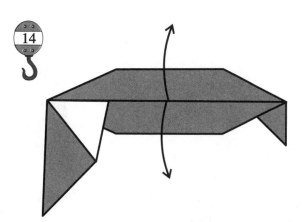

Open out the sides of the hull.

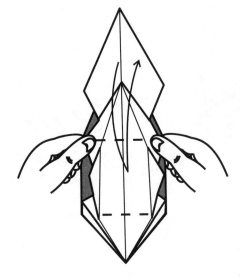

Grasp the sides of the hull and valley-fold between the corners and unfold. Repeat at the bottom.

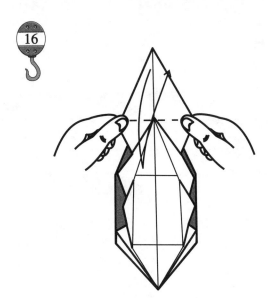

Grasp the sides of the sail, and valley-fold the model and unfold. This will keep the sail open. Adjust the rudder to point downward.

Side view of the Double-Ended Sailboat.

Top view of the Double-Ended Sailboat.

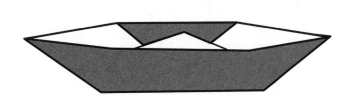

Lifeboat

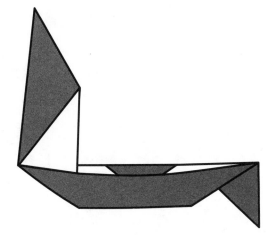

Double-Ended Sailboat

This sailboat now has the necessary parts to sail on a straight course.

Sailboat Sails

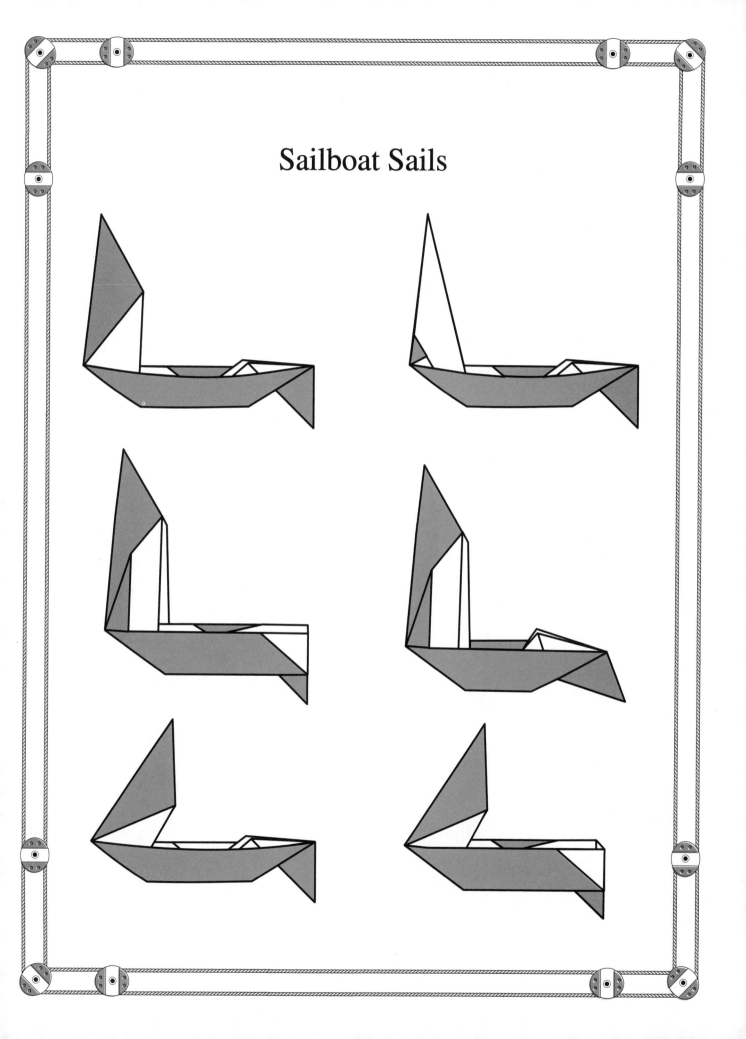

Sailboat in Starboard Sail

When you are facing the front or bow from within the boat, the right side is called the starboard and the left side is called the port. Sails can be set on the starboard side or the port side of a sailboat. Each setting will make the boat sail differently.

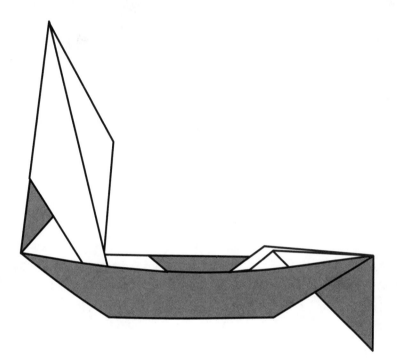

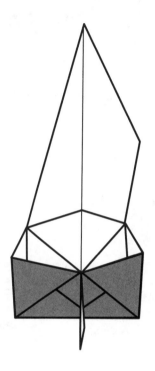

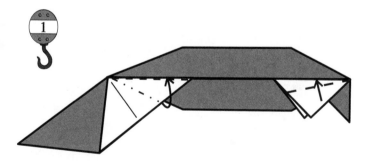

Begin with step 12 of the Double-Ended Sailboat (page 39). Swivel the near half of the sail up into the model. Valley-fold the near right flap upward tucking it up as far as possible into the hull.

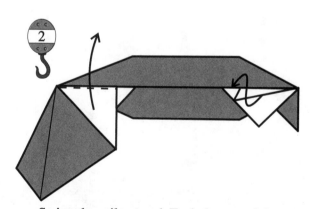

Swing the sail upward. Tuck the near right flap, still pointed downward, inside the lower half of the hull.

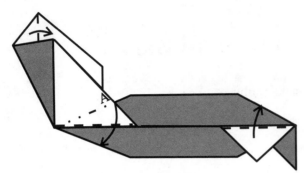

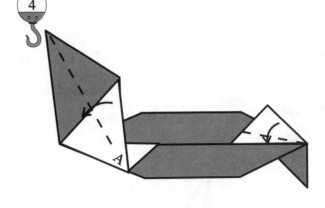

Pull corner A clockwise onto the near side of the hull. Swing the small triangular flap upward.

Valley-fold only the near right edge of the sail to the far left. Valley-fold the near right flap as far as possible down into the hull.

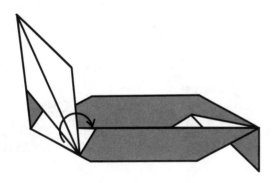

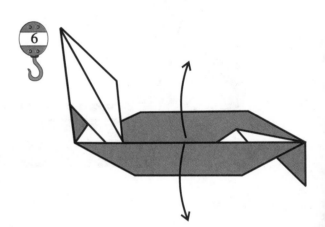

Tuck the base of the sail down into the hull. The sail is asymmetrical.

Open out the sides of the hull.

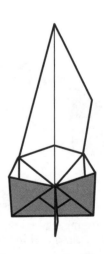

The completed Sailboat in Starboard Sail.

View from rear of sailboat.

Sailboat in Port Sail

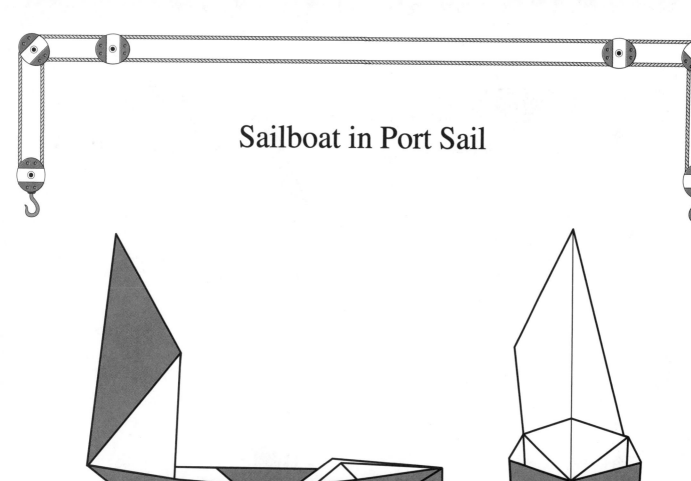

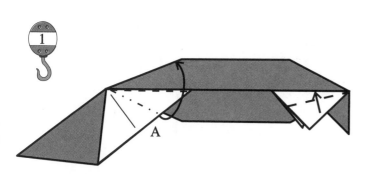

Begin with step 12 of the Double-Ended
Sailboat (page 39). Swivel the near half of the
sail counterclockwise over the hull and flatten;
watch spot A. Valley-fold the near right flap up
into the model as far as possible. The small area
remaining visible is called a coaming.

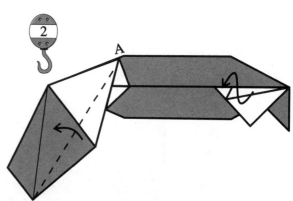

Valley-fold the near right edge of the sail leftward to the
vertical crease. Then open the hull at the right and place
the finished coaming, still pointed downward, inside the
lower half of the hull.

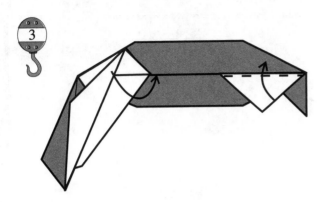

Tuck the upper part of the sail inside the hull. Swing the right flap upward.

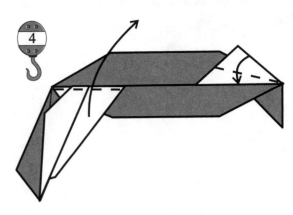

Valley-fold the sail upward. Valley-fold the right flap down into the hull as far as possible to form the second coaming.

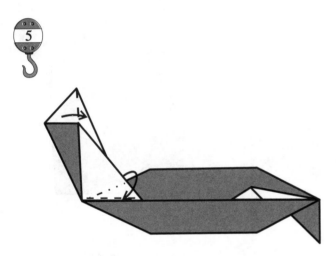

Swivel the near half of the sail down into the hull and flatten the model. The sail is asymmetrical; it is narrower in the back than in the front.

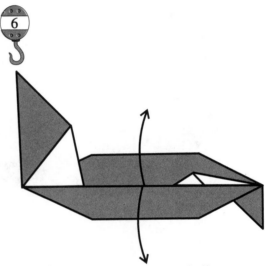

Open out the sides of the hull.

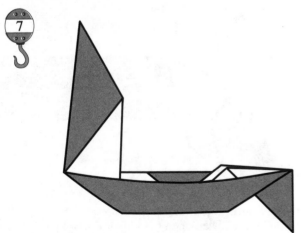

The completed Sailboat in Port Sail. Coamings help keep water out of the sailboat. The area inside the sailboat above the rudder is called the cockpit.

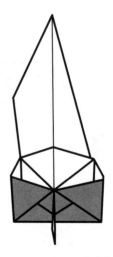

Here is a view from behind.

Sailboat in Half Sail

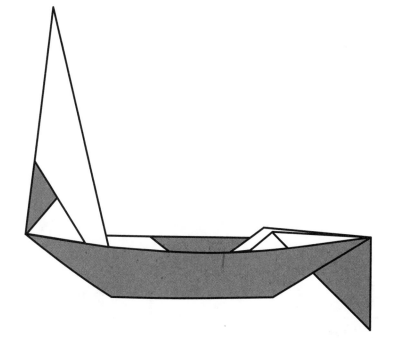

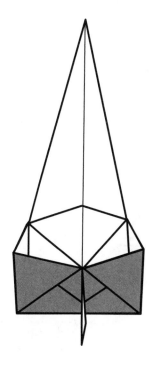

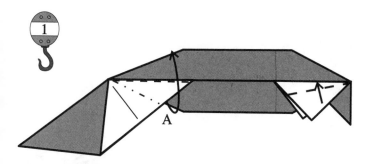

1

Begin with step 12 of the Double-Ended
Sailboat (page 39). Swivel the near half of the
sail counterclockwise over the hull and flatten;
watch spot A. Valley-fold the near right flap
upward, tucking it as far as possible into the
hull.

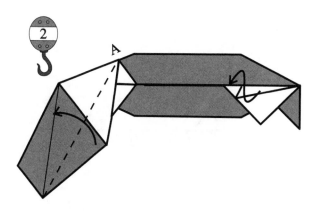

2

Valley-fold the near right edge of the sail
leftward to the vertical crease. Then open
the hull at the right and place the finished
coaming, still pointed downward, inside
the lower half of the hull.

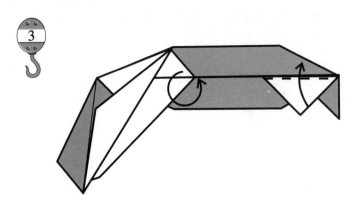

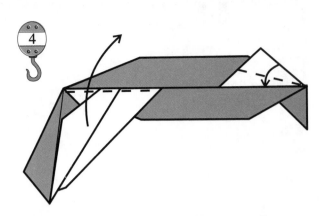

Tuck the upper part of the sail inside the hull. Swing the right flap upward.

Valley-fold the sail upward. Valley-fold the right flap down into the hull as far as possible to form the second coaming.

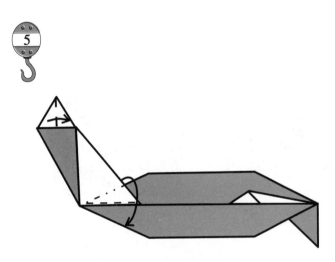

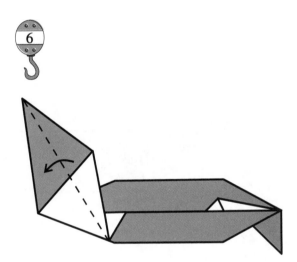

Swivel the near half of the sail down clockwise down onto the near side of the hull and flatten the model. The sail is asymmetrical in step 6.

Repeat step 2 on the near half of the sail. Then tuck the lower part of the sail inside the hull.

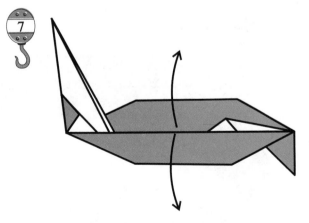

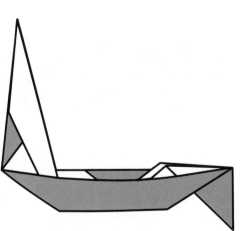

Open out the sides of the hull.

Here is a view from behind.

The completed Sailboat in Half Sail. The half sail is used when the wind is too strong for a full sail.

Sailboat Sail Angles

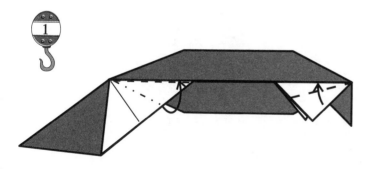

Begin with step 12 of the Double-Ended Sailboat (page 39). Swivel the near half of the sail counterclockwise into the hull and flatten. Valley-fold the near right flap up into the model as far as possible. The small area remaining visible is called a coaming.

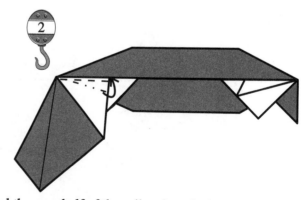

Swivel the near half of the sail up into the hull again. Repeat steps 1 and 2 behind. You can adjust the angle by folding less paper into the model. Complete the coamings as in the two previous models.

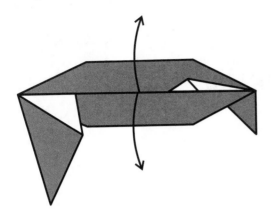

Open out the sides of the hull.

The completed Sailboat. By varying the amount of paper you fold into the model, you can produce different angles to accomodate the amount of wind. In a heavy wind you may want to use a more acute angle to keep the sailboat from overturning.

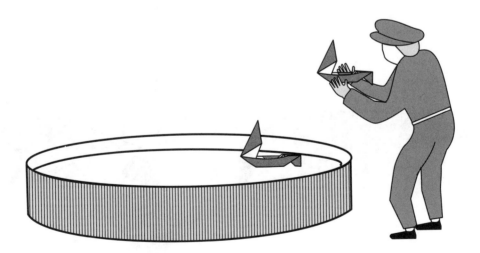

Skysail Sailboat

Sailboats often have additional sails which increase the height of sail. These are sometimes called Skysails.

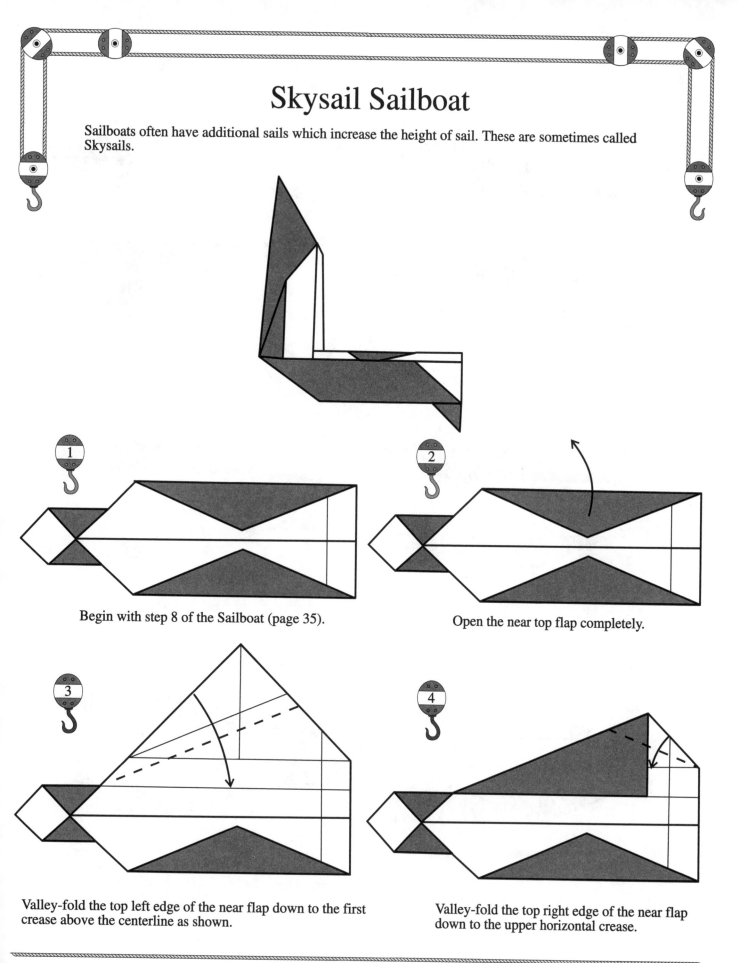

Begin with step 8 of the Sailboat (page 35).

Open the near top flap completely.

Valley-fold the top left edge of the near flap down to the first crease above the centerline as shown.

Valley-fold the top right edge of the near flap down to the upper horizontal crease.

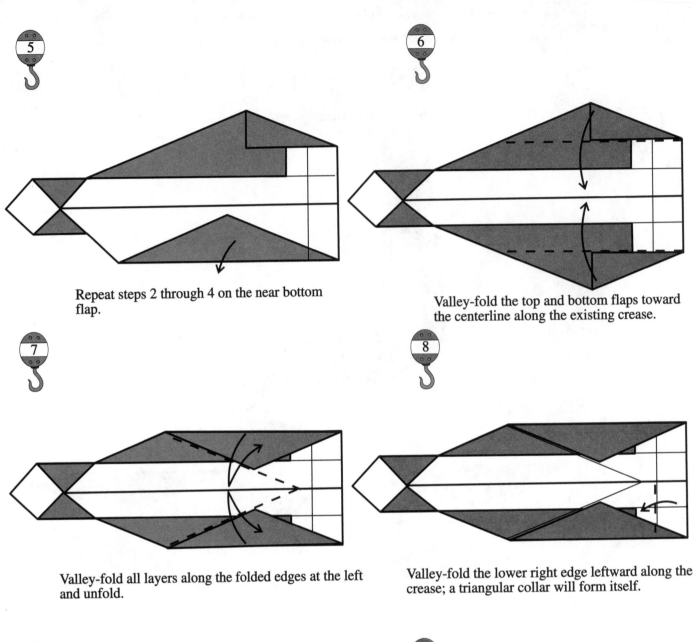

5 Repeat steps 2 through 4 on the near bottom flap.

6 Valley-fold the top and bottom flaps toward the centerline along the existing crease.

7 Valley-fold all layers along the folded edges at the left and unfold.

8 Valley-fold the lower right edge leftward along the crease; a triangular collar will form itself.

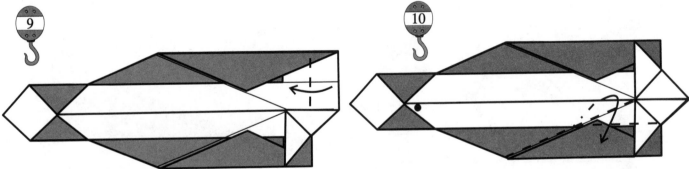

9 Repeat step 8 at the upper right.

10 Boat-fold the bottom left side. Pull the center edge downward in a boat-fold. The left flap will rise to begin formation of the sail. Watch the black dot.

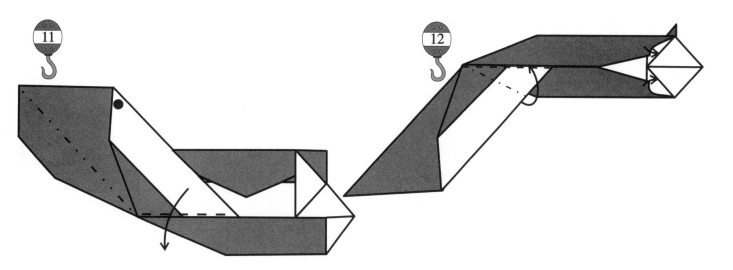

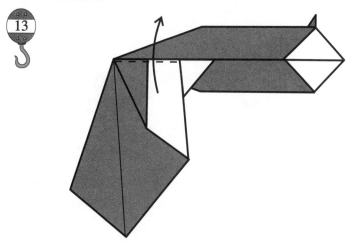

Valley-fold the left near flap down along the folded edge of the hull. Repeat step 10 on the top half. Although the flap is larger than that of the Sailboat, the folding remains the same.

Swivel the near half of the sail up into the hull and flatten. Tuck the inner right corners into the triangular pockets behind them.

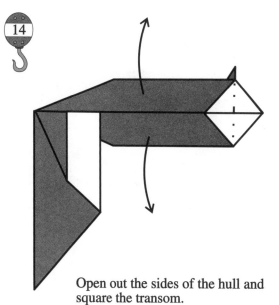

Swing the sail upward and repeat step 12. Flatten the sail downward.

Open out the sides of the hull and square the transom.

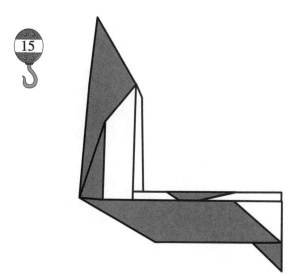

Side view of the Skysail Sailboat.

Double-Ended Skysail Sailboat

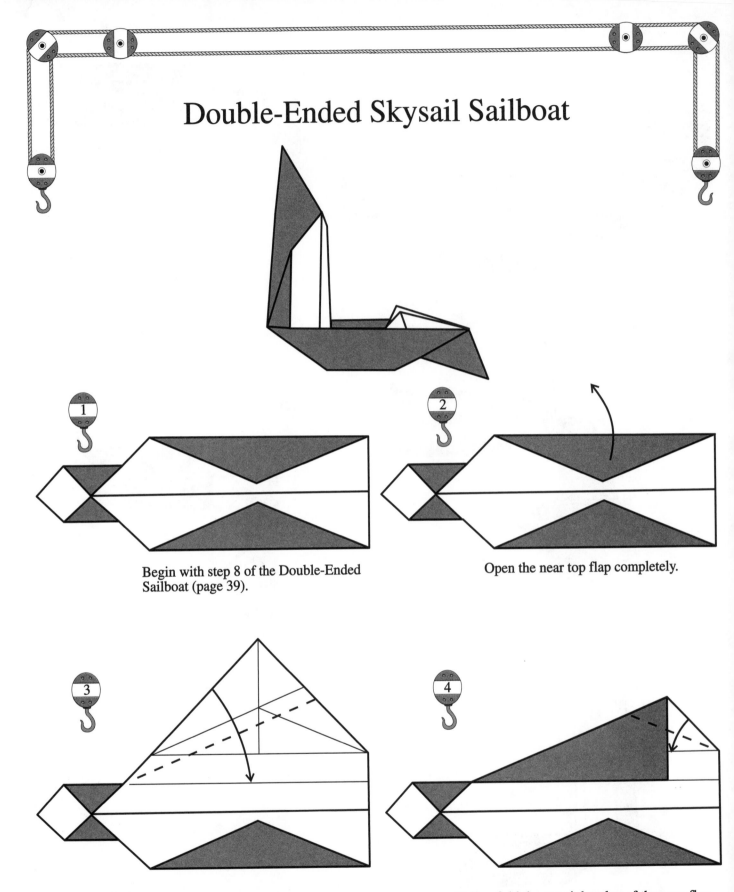

1

Begin with step 8 of the Double-Ended Sailboat (page 39).

2

Open the near top flap completely.

3

Valley-fold the top left edge of the near flap down to the first crease above the centerline as shown.

4

Valley-fold the top right edge of the near flap down to the upper horizontal crease.

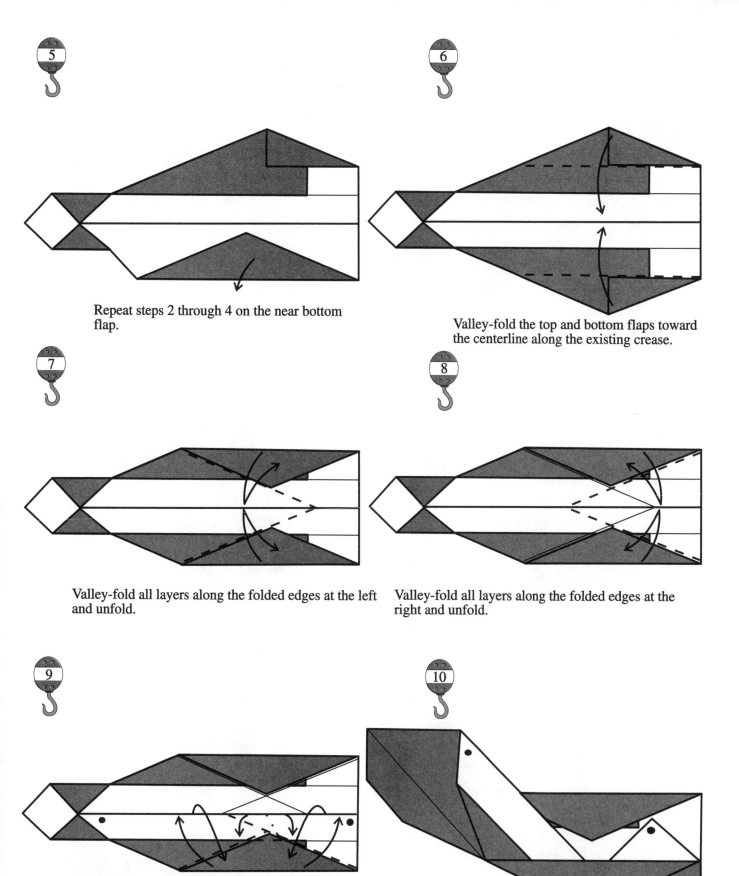

5

Repeat steps 2 through 4 on the near bottom flap.

6

Valley-fold the top and bottom flaps toward the centerline along the existing crease.

7

Valley-fold all layers along the folded edges at the left and unfold.

8

Valley-fold all layers along the folded edges at the right and unfold.

9

Working from the right, boat-fold the lower half; the left boat-fold construction will overlap the one on the right. Watch the black dots.

10

The large left flap becomes a skysail.

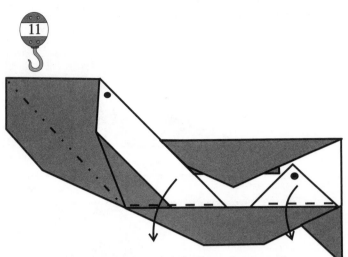

11

Valley-fold the near left and right flaps downward.
Boat-fold the top half of the sailboat.

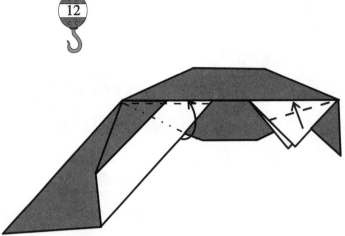

12

Swivel the near half of the sail up into the hull.
Valley-fold the near right flap up into the model to
form the stern and coaming.

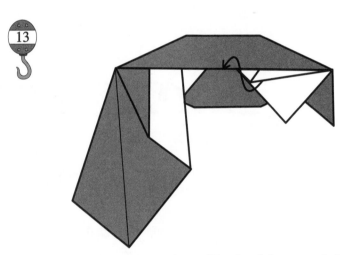

13

Tuck the finished coaming, still pointed downward, down
inside the lower half of the hull.

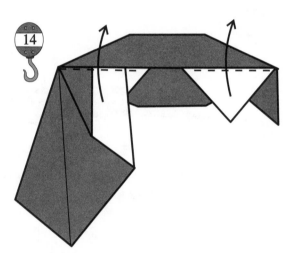

14

Valley-fold the near left and right flaps upward.
Repeat step 12. Flatten the sail downward.

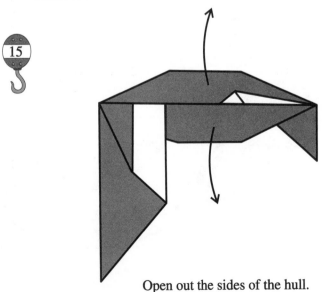

15

Open out the sides of the hull.

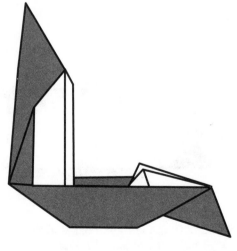

Side view of the Double-Ended Skysail Sailboat.

Sailboat Rudders

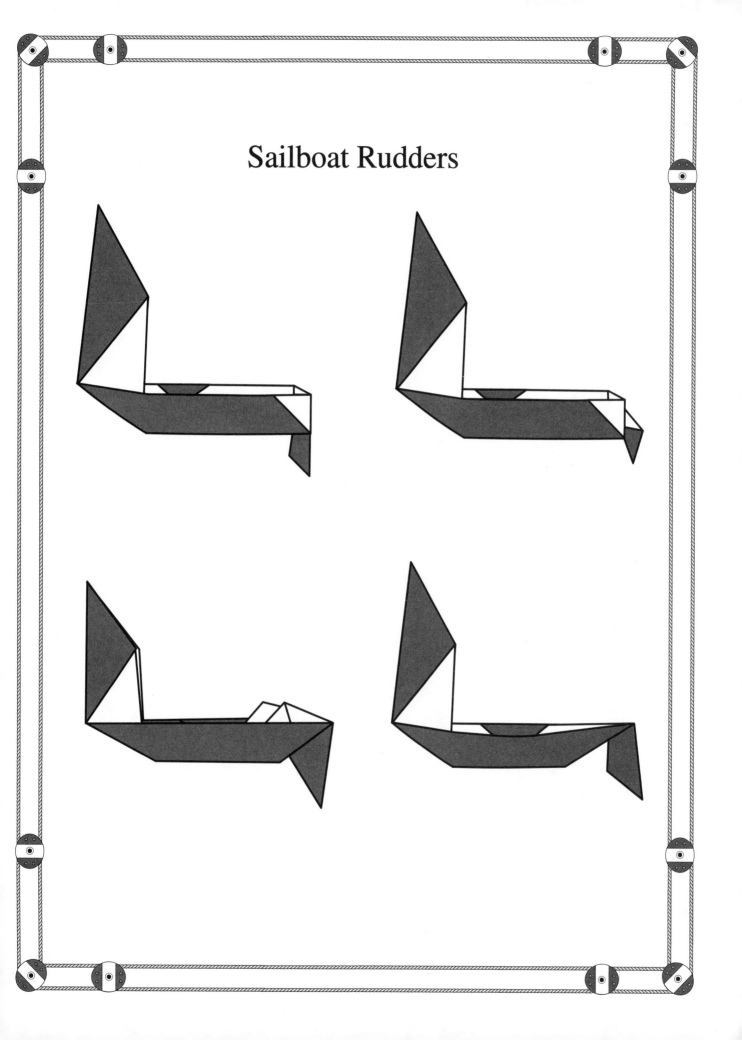

Sailboat with a Small Rudder

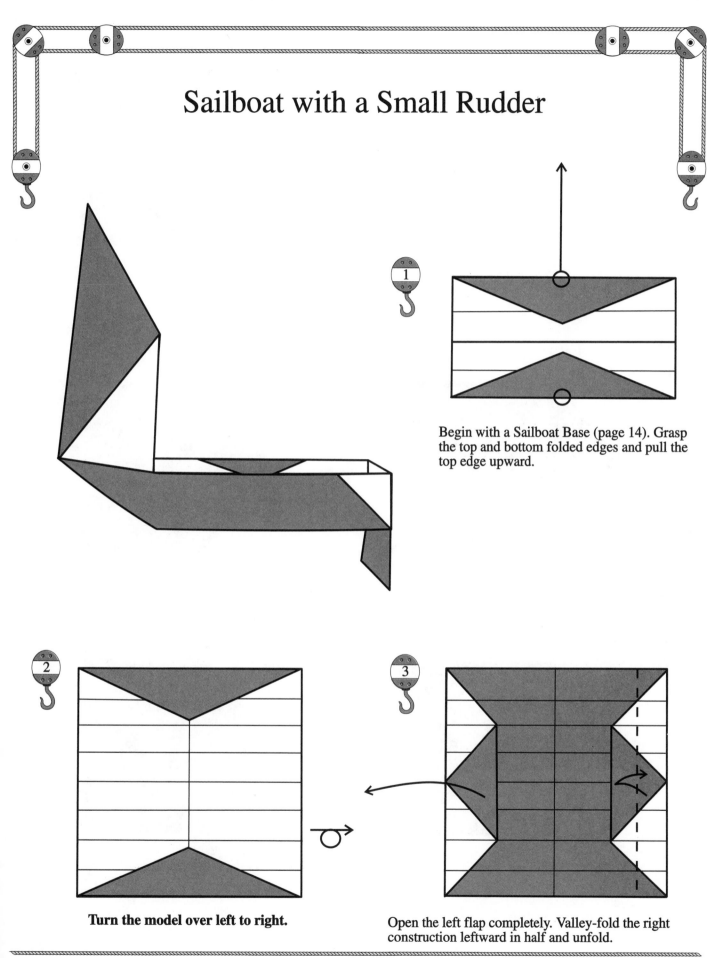

1 Begin with a Sailboat Base (page 14). Grasp the top and bottom folded edges and pull the top edge upward.

2 **Turn the model over left to right.**

3 Open the left flap completely. Valley-fold the right construction leftward in half and unfold.

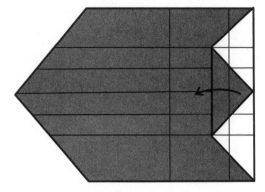

Unfold the near right flap.

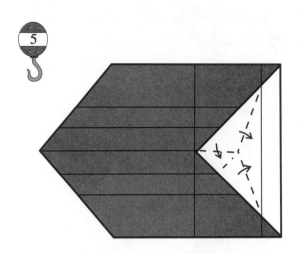

Rabbit-ear the near flap to the crease formed in step 3.

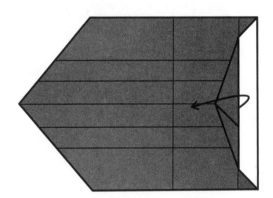

Unfold the rabbit ear.

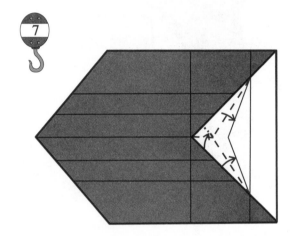

Rabbit-ear the near flap to the creases formed in step 5.

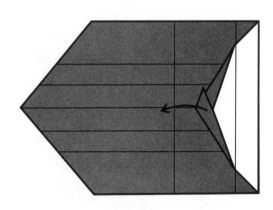

Unfold.

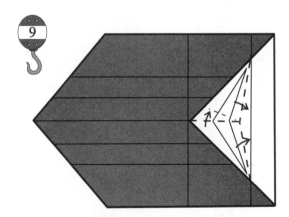

Rabbit-ear the near right flap so that the creases folded in step 5 are vertical; they will lie on the long vertical crease formed in step 3.

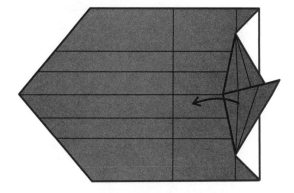

Unfold.

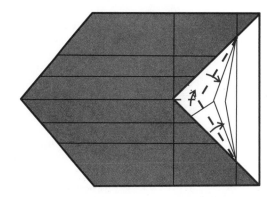

Rabbit-ear the near flap on the creases formed in step 7.

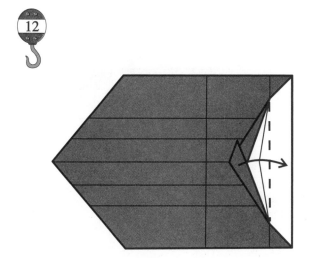

Swing the entire near right flap to the right, along the existing vertical crease.

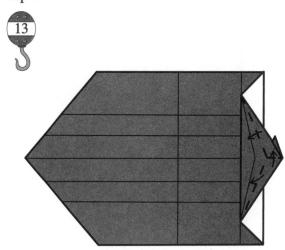

Rabbit-ear the near right flap along the rightmost rabbit ear crease lines.

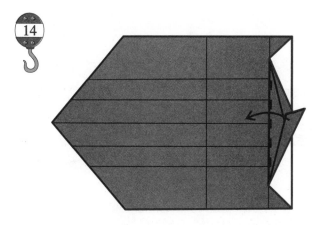

Swing the right flap to the left.

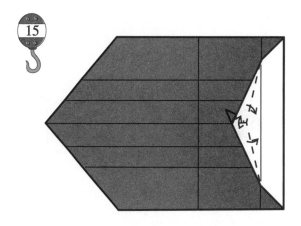

Rabbit-ear the near right flap rightward to the vertical crease.

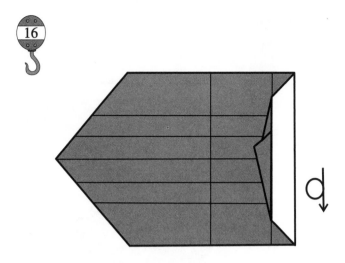

Turn the model over.

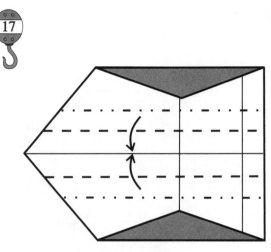

Refold the center of the model as shown. (The result will look like step 18.)

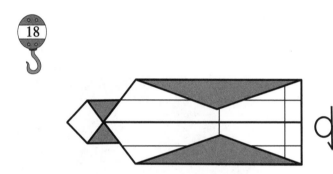

Turn the model over.

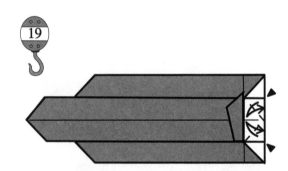

Valley-fold the near right inner corners to the centerline, and then unfold them. Reverse-fold the corners into the model.

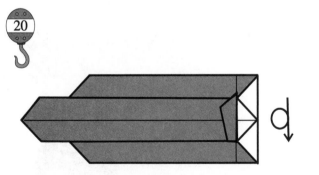

Turn the model over.

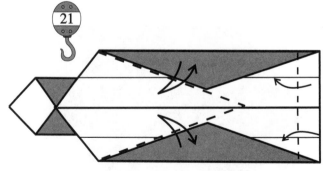

Enlarged view. Valley-fold and unfold all layers at the left along the folded edges of the near flaps. Then valley-fold the bottom right corner to the left along the existing crease. A triangular collar will form itself. Repeat on the top right corner.

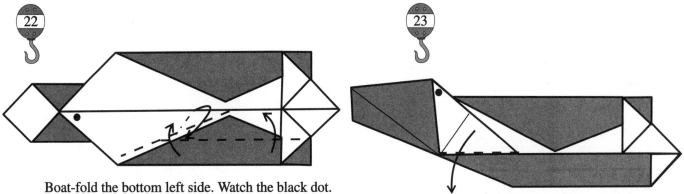

22 Boat-fold the bottom left side. Watch the black dot.

23 Swing the sail downward enough to open the model. Then boat-fold the upper half. Flatten the sail downward.

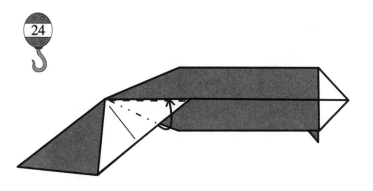

24 Swivel the near half of the sail up into the hull.

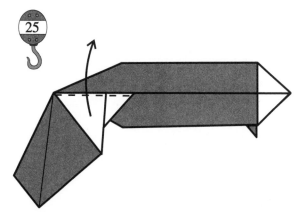

25 Swing the sail upward and repeat step 24. Flatten the sail downward.

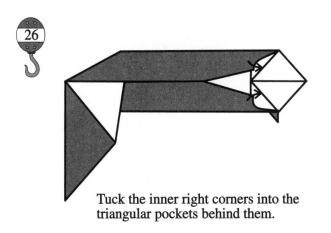

26 Tuck the inner right corners into the triangular pockets behind them.

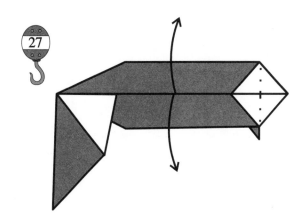

27 Open sides of the hull. Square off the transom.

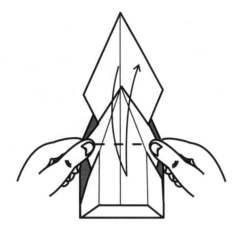

Grasp the sides of the hull and valley-fold between the corners and unfold.

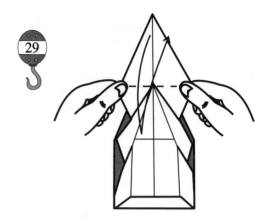

Grasp the sides of the sail, and valley-fold it and unfold. This will keep the sail open.

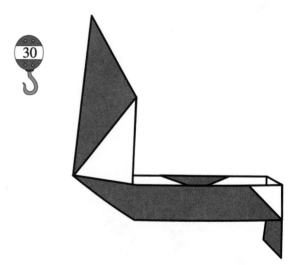

Side view of the Sailboat with a Small Rudder.

Sailboat with an Outboard Rudder

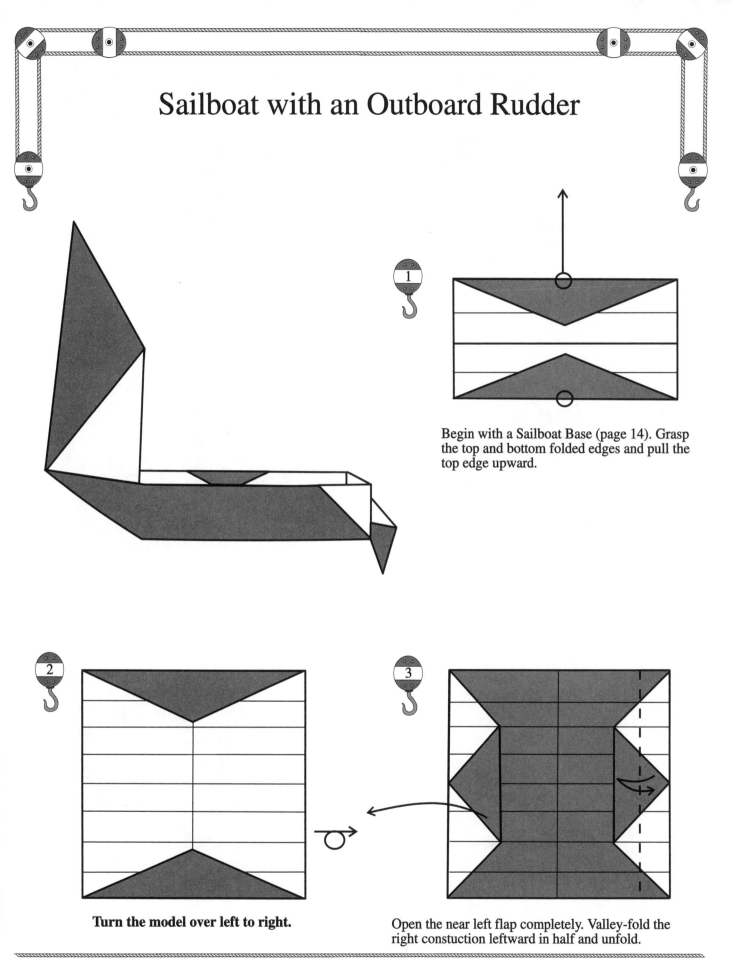

1 Begin with a Sailboat Base (page 14). Grasp the top and bottom folded edges and pull the top edge upward.

2 **Turn the model over left to right.**

3 Open the near left flap completely. Valley-fold the right constuction leftward in half and unfold.

4

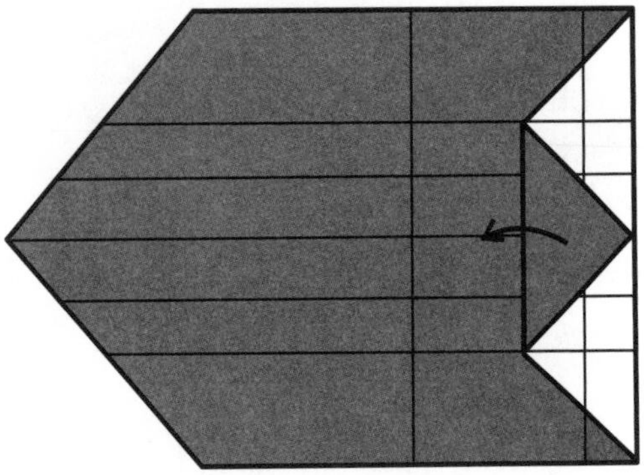

Unfold the near right flap.

5

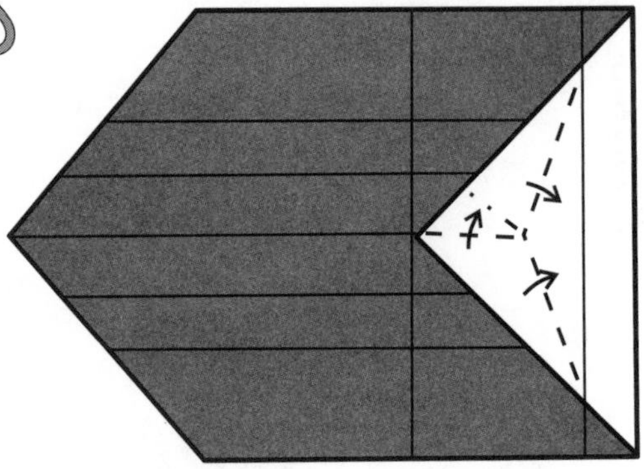

Rabbit-ear the near flap to the crease formed in step 3.

6

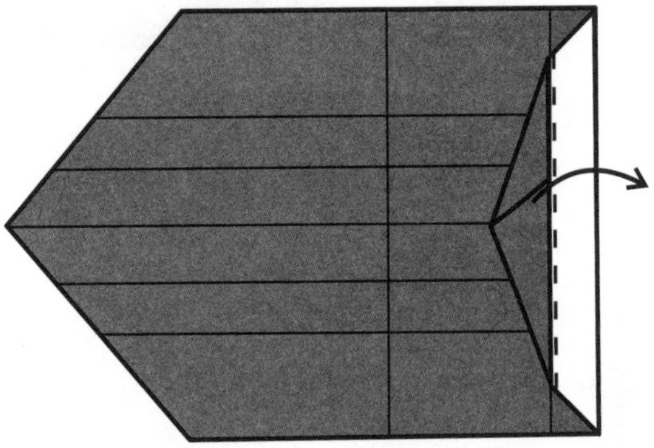

Valley-fold the rabbit ear construction to the right along the existing crease.

7

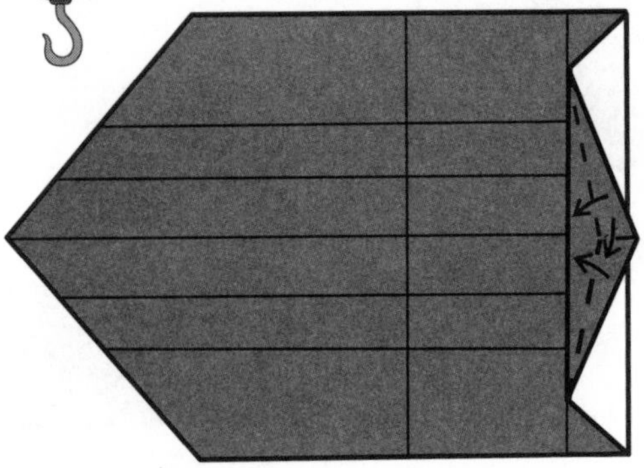

Form a rabbit ear of the rabbit ear construction.

8

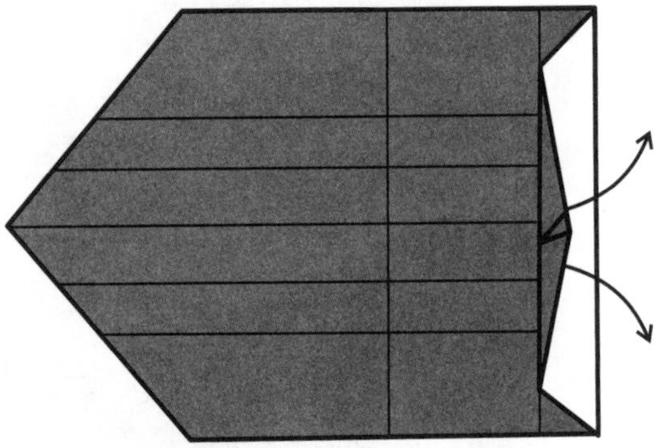

Reach under the flap from the right and gently pull out its raw edges.

9

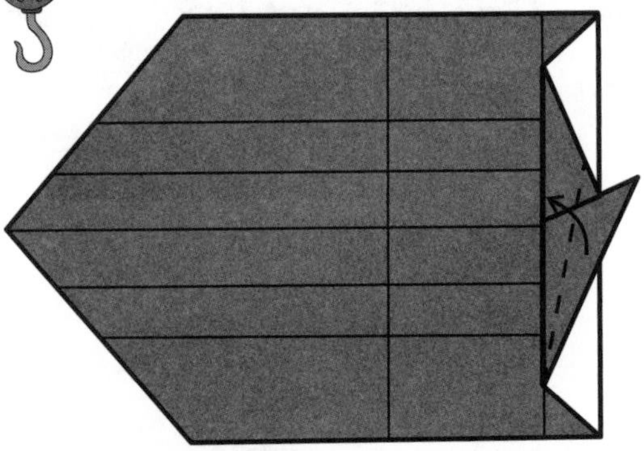

Valley-fold the near flap in half.

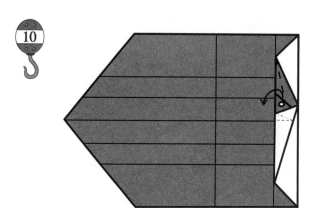

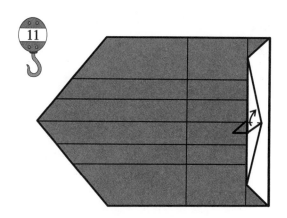

Place your left thumbprint behind the small triangular flap and grasp it between thumb and index finger; then twist the flap away from yourself in a corkscrew motion. Bring it down as far as it will comfortably go, while you valley-fold leftward the upper edge of the colored flap.

Swing the small flap upward.

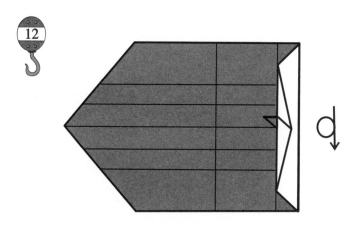

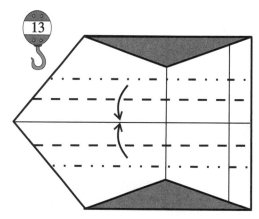

Turn the model over.

Refold the valley and mountain folds in the center of the model so that it looks like step 14.

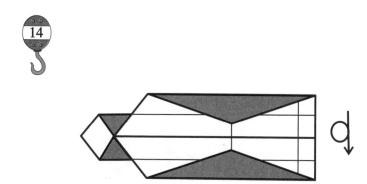

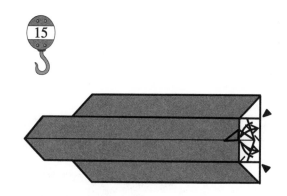

Turn the model over.

Valley-fold and unfold the near right inner corners to the centerline; then reverse-fold them into the model.

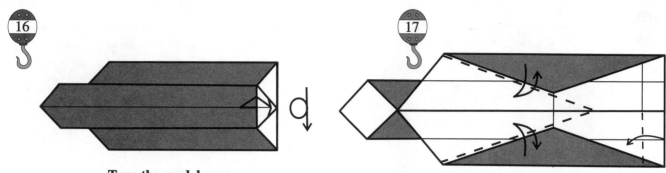

Turn the model over.

Enlarged view. Valley-fold and unfold at the left along the folded edges of the near flaps. Then valley-fold the bottom right corner leftward along the crease formed in step 3.

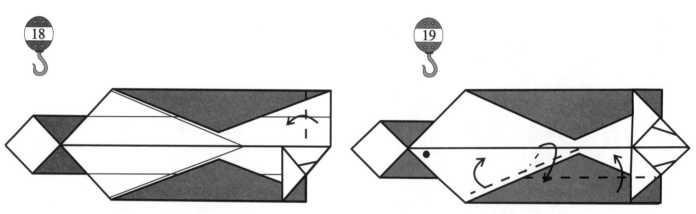

Repeat step 17 on the top right corner.

Boat-fold the bottom left side. Watch the black dot.

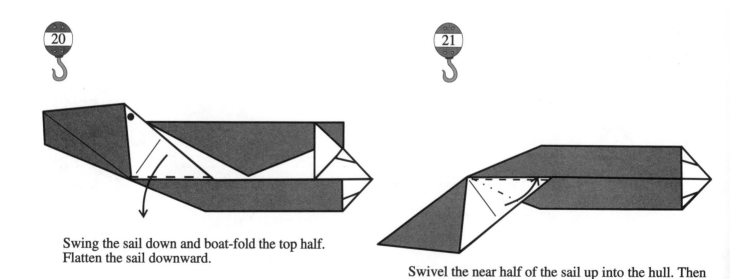

Swing the sail down and boat-fold the top half. Flatten the sail downward.

Swivel the near half of the sail up into the hull. Then swing the sail upward and repeat these actions on the remaining half. Flatten the sail downward.

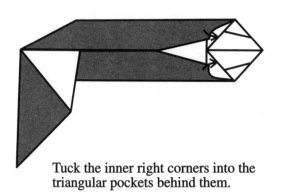

Tuck the inner right corners into the triangular pockets behind them.

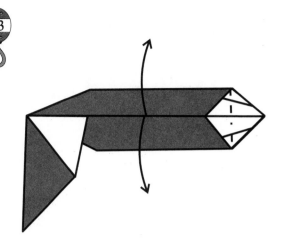

Open the sides of the hull. Square off the transom.

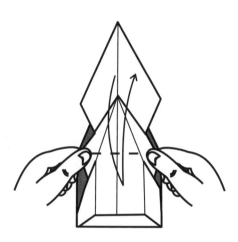

Grasp the sides of the hull and valley-fold between the corners and unfold.

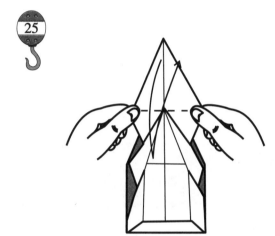

Grasp the sides of the sail, and valley-fold and unfold. This will keep the sail open.

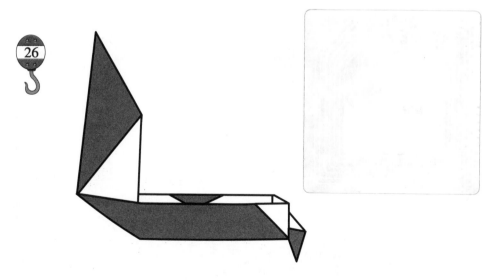

Side view of the Sailboat with an Outboard Rudder.

Double-Ended Sailboat with a Large Rudder

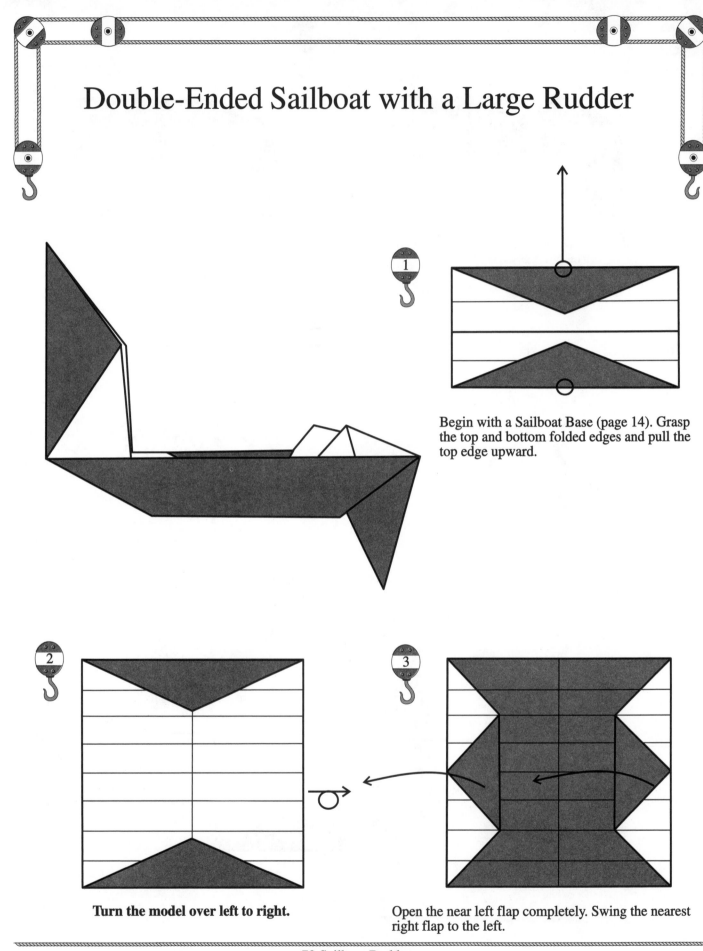

1 Begin with a Sailboat Base (page 14). Grasp the top and bottom folded edges and pull the top edge upward.

2 **Turn the model over left to right.**

3 Open the near left flap completely. Swing the nearest right flap to the left.

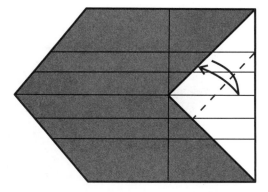

Valley-fold the right near flap: the fold line should run from from the crease just below the centerline to the second crease above the centerline. Unfold.

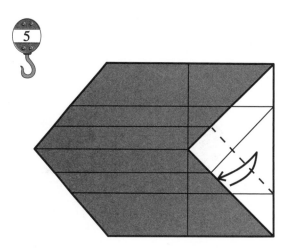

Repeat step 4 on the lower part of the near flap.

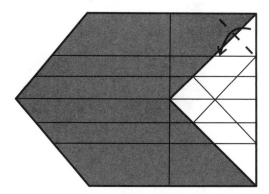

Valley-fold the upper right corner to the second crease from the centerline.

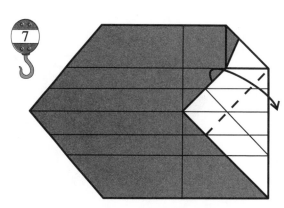

Valley-fold the near flap along the crease formed in step 4, gently pulling out the inner portion of the near right corner.

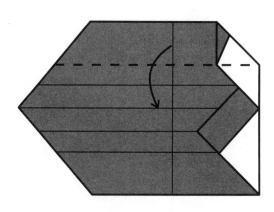

Valley-fold the upper edge down along the second crease from the centerline.

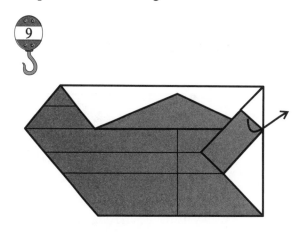

Gently bring out the hidden paper from within the upper right corner; pull it as far as possible to the right and flatten the model.

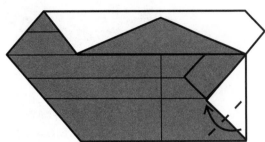

Repeat step 6 on the lower right corner.

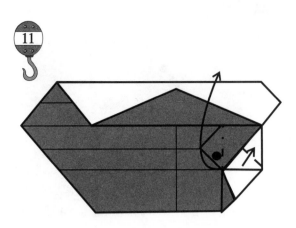

Pull to the top the dotted tip of the single-layer corner and flatten; watch the black dot. The paper hidden within the lower right corner will automatically be pulled out. Flatten the model.

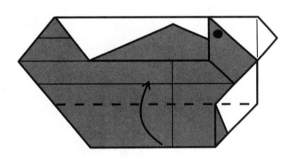

Valley-fold the lower edge up along the second crease from the centerline.

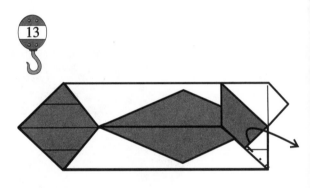

Gently bring out the paper from within the lower right corner. Pull it as far as possible to the right and flatten the model.

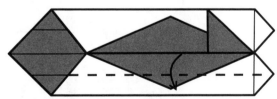

Valley-fold the central edge of the lower half down to the botttom.

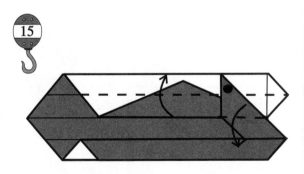

Swing the dotted flap downward; this will be the rudder. Repeat step 14 on the upper half of the model.

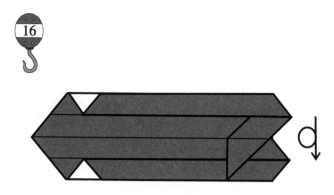

Turn the model over.

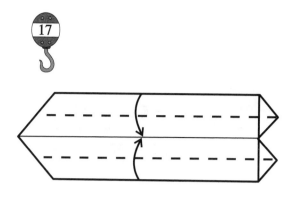

Swing the upper and lower near edges to
the centerline. Look ahead to step 18.

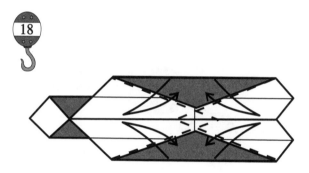

Valley-fold and unfold at the left along the edges of the
near flaps. Repeat on the right side of the model.

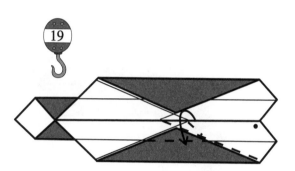

Boat-fold the bottom right side. Watch the black dot.

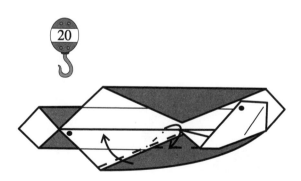

Boat-fold the bottom left side. The large dotted flap will rise
to become the sail. Flatten the model.

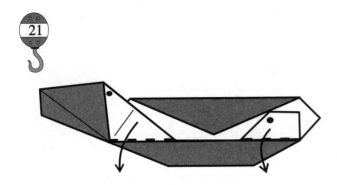

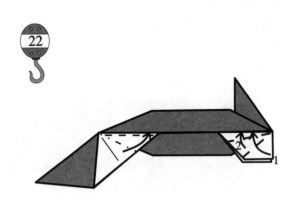

Valley-fold down the near left and right flaps to expose the top half of the model. Repeat steps 19 and 20 on the top half.

Swivel the near layers of the sail into the model. Valley-fold the near right flap twice and tuck it up into the model.

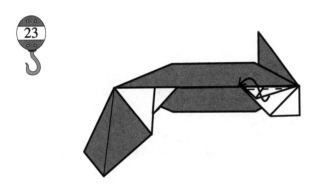

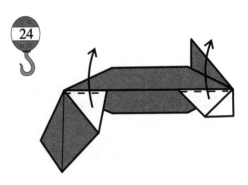

Tuck the finished coaming, still pointed downward, down into the hull.

Swing the left and right flaps upward and repeat step 22. Flatten the sail downward.

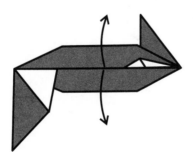

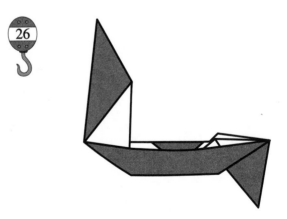

Open out the sides of the hull.

Double-Ended Sailboat with a Large Rudder.

Double-Ended Sailboat with a Small Rudder

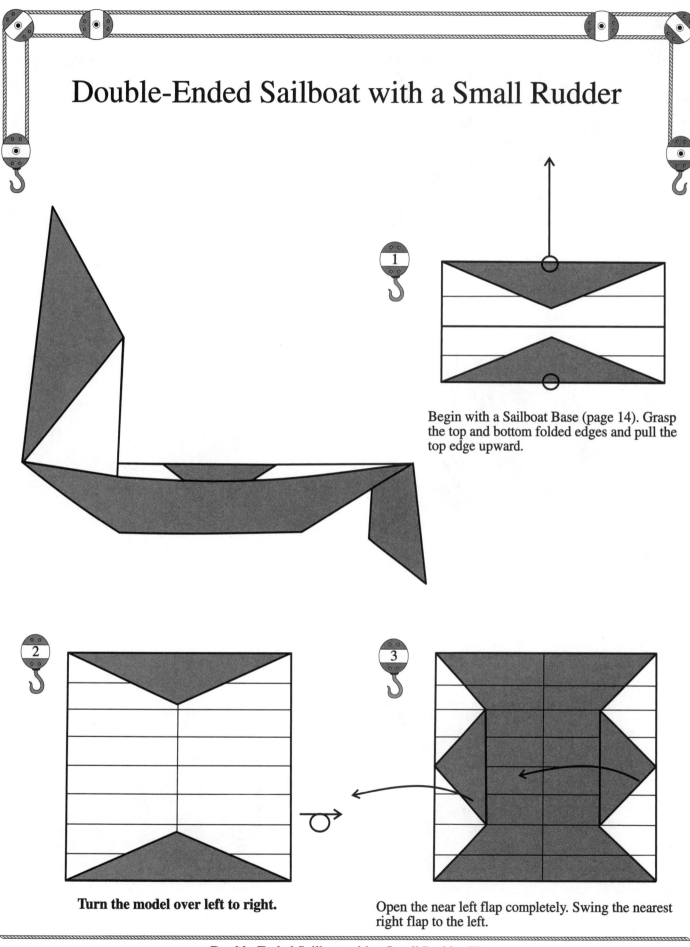

1

Begin with a Sailboat Base (page 14). Grasp the top and bottom folded edges and pull the top edge upward.

2

Turn the model over left to right.

3

Open the near left flap completely. Swing the nearest right flap to the left.

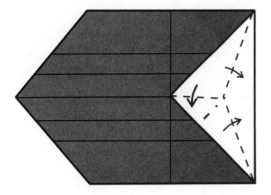

Rabbit-ear the near flap.

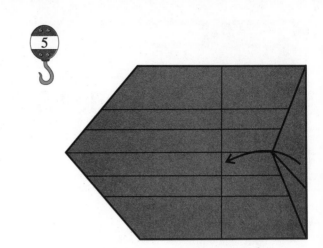

Unfold.

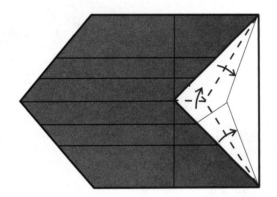

Rabbit-ear the near flap over to the creases formed in step 4.

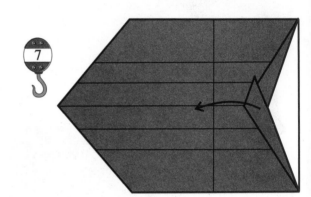

Unfold.

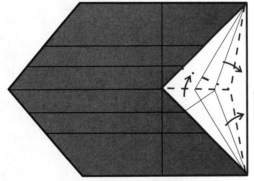

Rabbit-ear the near flap so that the creases folded in step 4 are vertical; they will lie along the vertical right edge of the model.

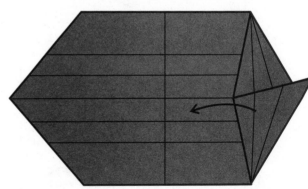

Unfold.

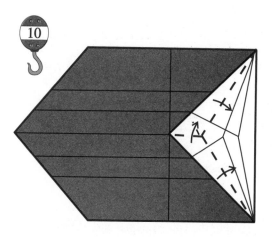

Rabbit-ear the near flap on the creases formed in step 6.

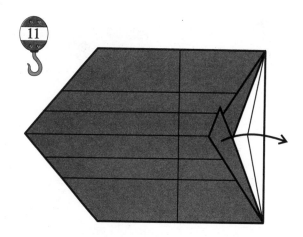

Swing the entire near flap to the right.

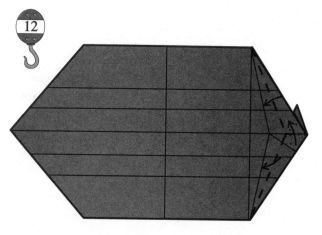

Rabbit-ear the near right flap leftward over to the creases formed in step 8.

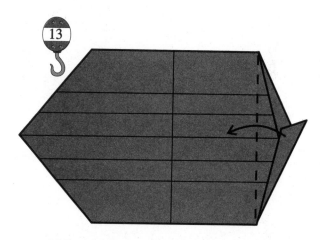

Valley-fold the right flap leftward along the existing vertical crease.

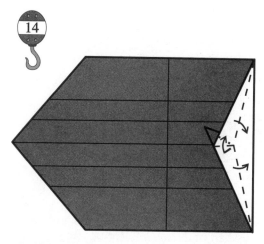

Rabbit-ear the near right flap rightward to the vertical folded edge.

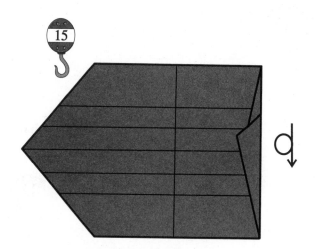

Turn the model over.

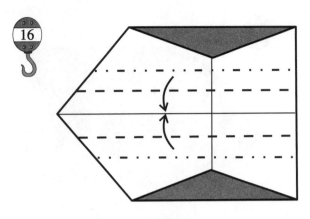

Refold as shown.

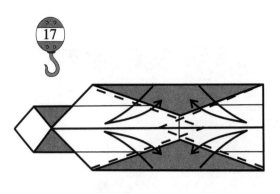

Valley-fold along the folded edges and unfold.

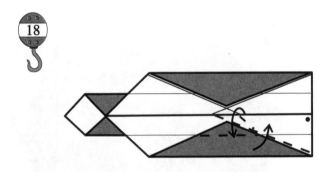

Boat-fold at the lower right. Watch the black dot.

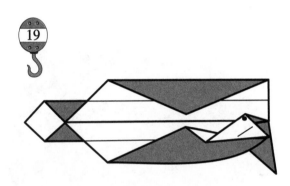

Step 19 shows this procedure in progress. Watch the black dot.

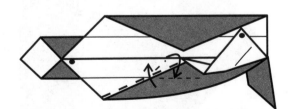

Boat-fold the bottom left side. Watch the black dot.

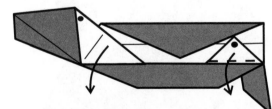

Swing down the near left and right flaps enough to expose the top half of the model. Repeat steps 18 through 20 to boat-fold the top half. Flatten the sail downward.

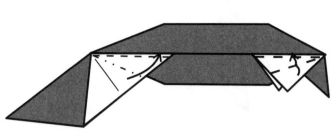

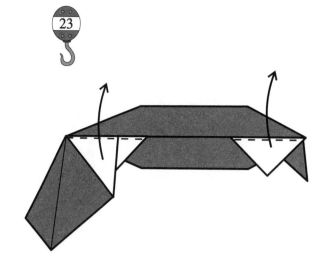

Swivel the near half of the sail up into the hull.
Valley-fold the near right flap up and tuck it into
the hull.

Swing the near left and right flaps upward and repeat step
22. Flatten the sail downward.

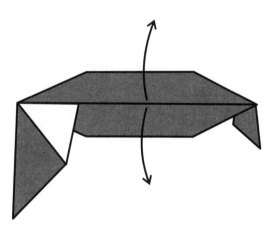

Open out the sides of the hull.

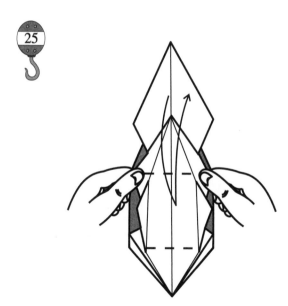

Grasp the sides of the hull and valley-fold
between the corners and unfold. Repeat at the
bottom.

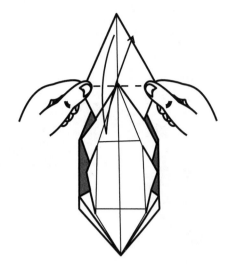

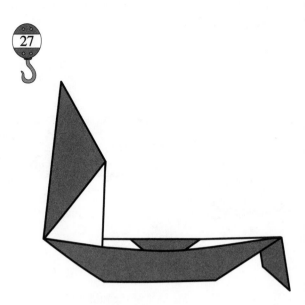

Grasp the sides of the sail; valley-fold the model and unfold. This will keep the sail open. Adjust the rudder so that it points downward.

Double-Ended Sailboat with a Small Rudder.

Sailboat Bows and Sterns

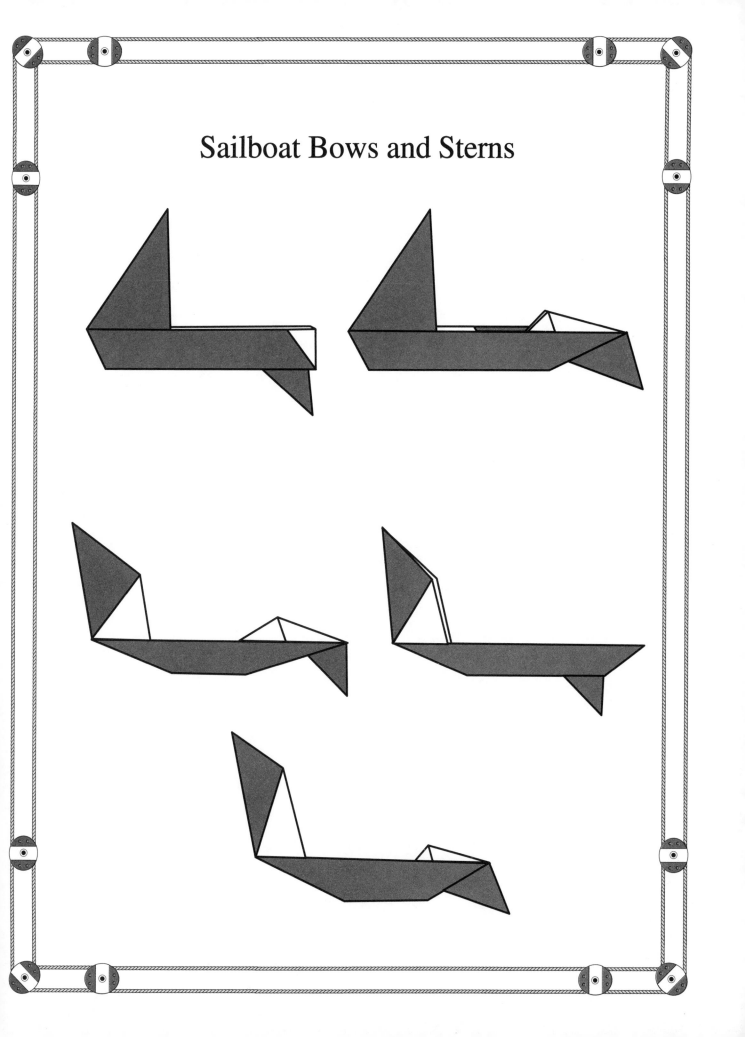

Short Raked-Bow Sailboat

Sailboats have bows and sterns that are made at different angles. Some have very short bows and long sterns. These angles on sailboats are called rakes.

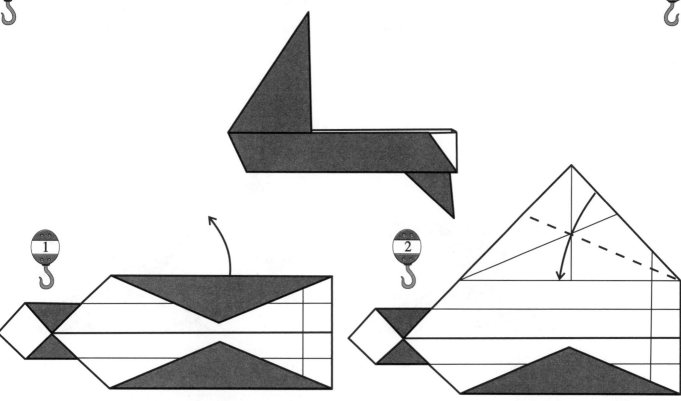

1 Begin with step 11 of the Sailboat (page 35). Open the near top flap completely.

2 Valley-fold the upper right edge down along the existing crease.

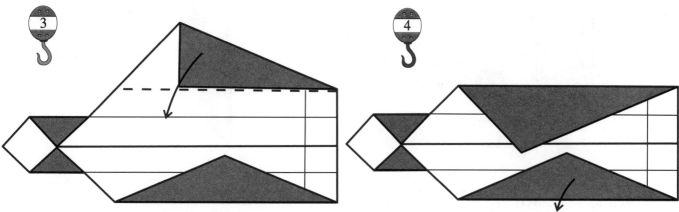

3 Valley-fold the top flap down along the existing horizontal crease.

4 Open the near lower flap completely and repeat steps 2 and 3.

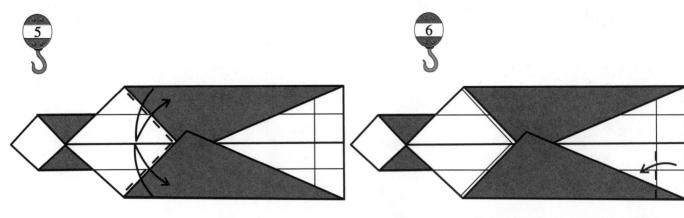

Valley-fold the upper and lower flaps along the folded edges and unfold.

Valley-fold the bottom right edge leftward along the existing crease. A triangular collar will form itself as the corner is flattened.

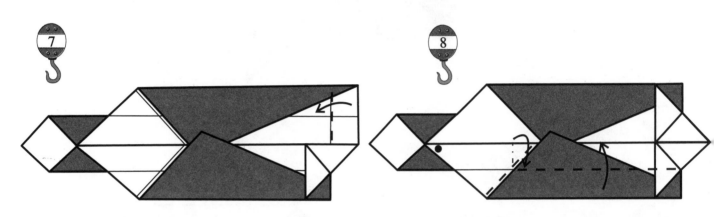

Repeat step 6 on the top right.

Boat-fold the bottom left flap. As you pull the white edge down clockwise, the black-dotted flap will begin to open into the sail. Note the vertical mountain-crease in this boat-fold; the white edge is pulled down into the hull as far as possible! Watch the black dot.

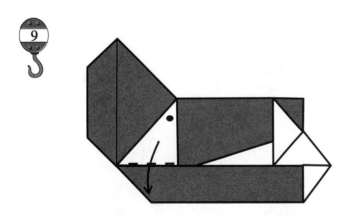

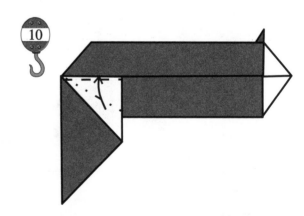

Swing the near left flap down along the centerline, opening the sail partway. Repeat step 8, boat-folding the top half. Flatten the sail downward.

Swivel the near half of the sail up into the hull, so that the sail's right edge is vertical in step 11.

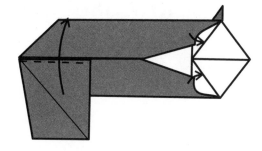

Valley-fold the sail upward and repeat step 10. Tuck the right inner corners into the triangular pockets behind them.

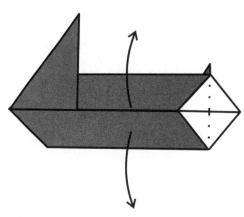

Open out the sides of the hull. Square the transom. Adjust the rudder to point downward.

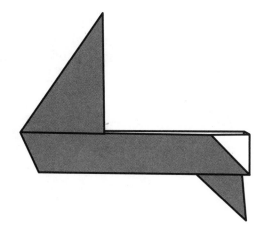

Side view of the Short Raked-Bow Sailboat.

Double-Ended Short Raked-Bow Sailboat

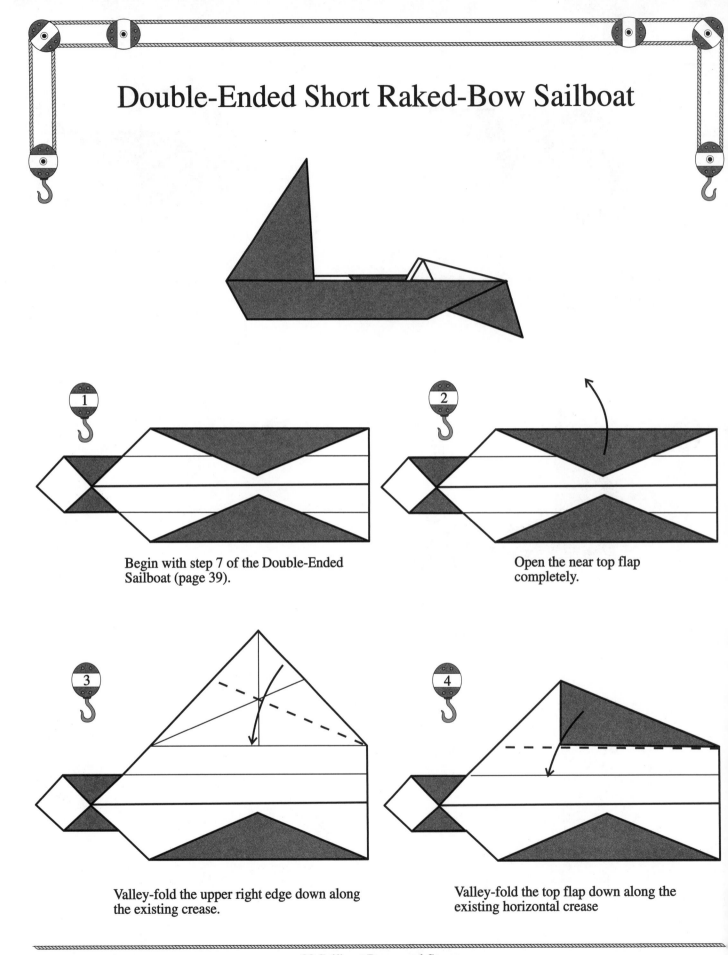

1 Begin with step 7 of the Double-Ended Sailboat (page 39).

2 Open the near top flap completely.

3 Valley-fold the upper right edge down along the existing crease.

4 Valley-fold the top flap down along the existing horizontal crease

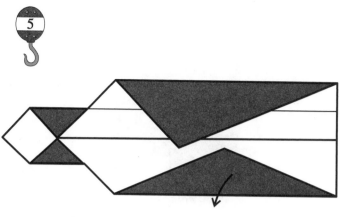

5

Repeat steps 2 through 4 on the near bottom flap.

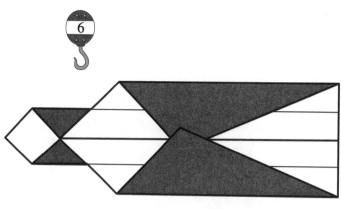

6

Although the newly formed flaps overlap the centerline, this will not interfere with the folding of the sailboat.

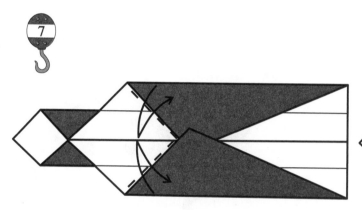

7

Valley-fold the upper and lower left flaps along the folded edges and unfold.

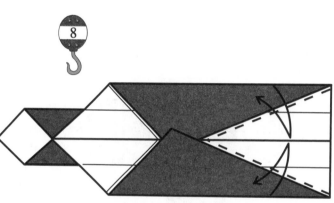

8

Valley-fold the upper and lower right flaps along the folded edges and unfold.

9

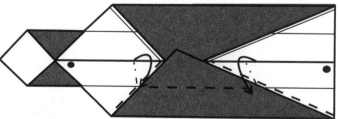

Boat-fold the lower left edge. Watch the black dot. As you pull the left white edge down clockwise, the black-dotted flap will begin to open into the sail. Note the vertical mountain-crease in the boat-fold; the white edge is pulled down into the hull as far as possible! Then boat-fold at the lower right. Watch the black dot.

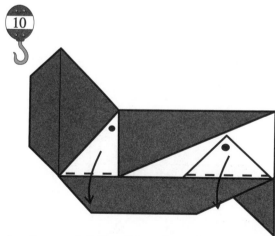

10

Swing the near left flap down along the centerline, opening the sail partway. Swing the triangular right flap downward. Then repeat step 9, boat-folding the top half. Flatten the sail downward.

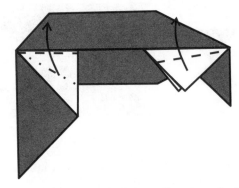

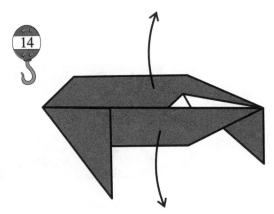

Swivel the near half of the sail up into the hull, so that the sail's right edge is vertical. Valley-fold the near triangular flap upward as far as possible into the hull to form a coaming.

Tuck the finished coaming, still pointed downward, down into the lower half of the hull.

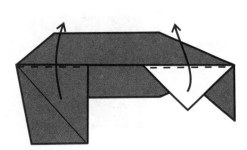

Swing both the sail and the small triangular flap upward. Repeat step 11. Flatten the sail downward.

Open out the sides of the hull.

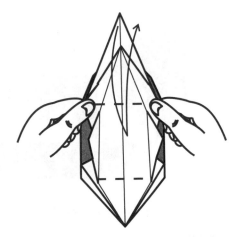

Grasp the sides of the hull and valley-fold between the corners and unfold. Repeat at the bottom. Adjust the rudder to point downward.

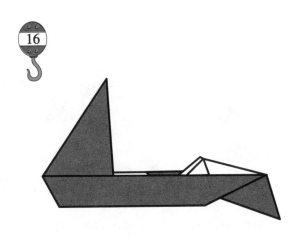

Side view of the Double-Ended Short Raked-Bow Sailboat.

Double-Ended Long Raked-Bow Sailboat

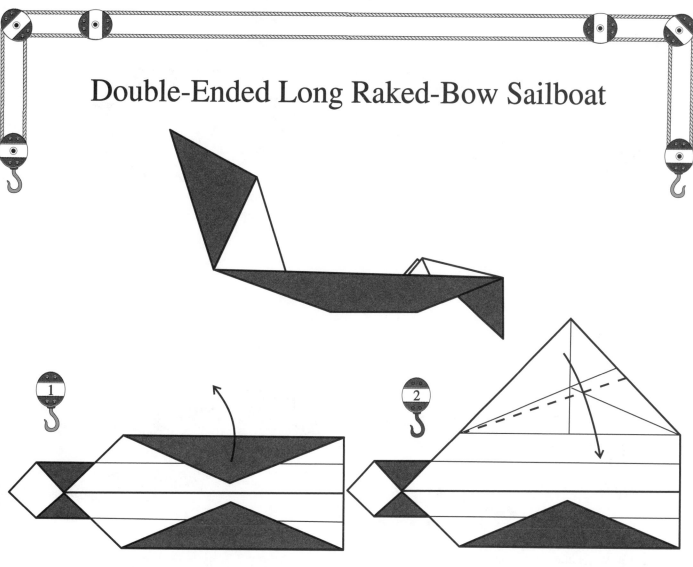

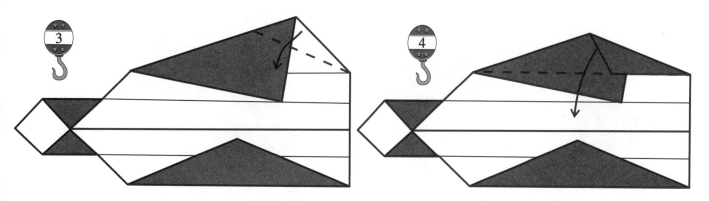

1 Begin with step 11 of the Sailboat (page 35). Open the near top flap completely.

2 Valley-fold the upper left edge down so that its tip touches the horizontal crease nearest the centerline.

3 Valley-fold the top flap down along the existing crease.

4 Valley-fold the top flap downward; the crease is horizontal.

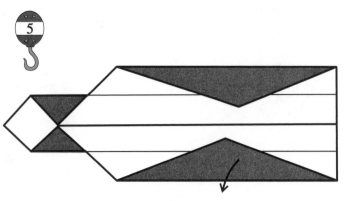

Repeat steps 1 through 4 on the near lower flap.

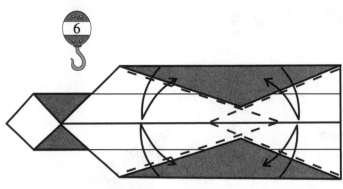

Valley-fold the upper and lower left flaps along the folded edges and unfold. Then valley-fold the upper and lower right flaps along the folded edges and unfold.

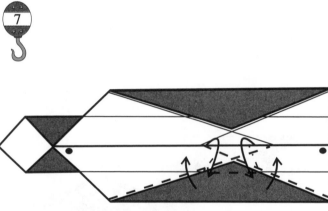

Now boat-fold both ends at once. The center portion will overlap. Watch the black dots.

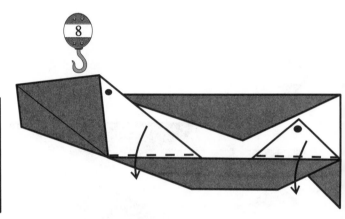

Swing the near left flap down along the centerline, opening the sail partway. Swing the small triangular flap downward. Then boat-fold the top half. Flatten the sail downward.

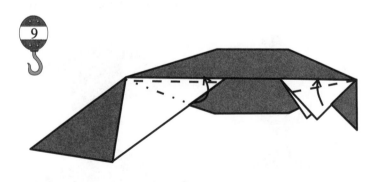

Swivel the near half of the sail up into the hull. Then valley-fold the near right flap up into the hull to form a coaming.

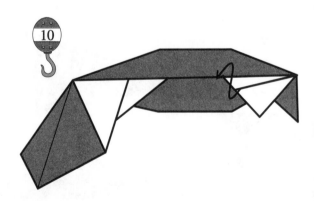

Tuck the finished coaming, still pointed downward, down into the lower half of the hull.

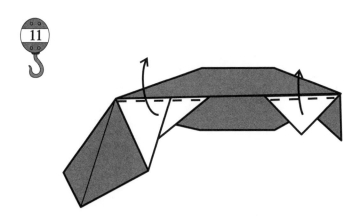

Swing the sail and the triangular flap upward. Repeat the actions of step 9. Flatten the sail downward.

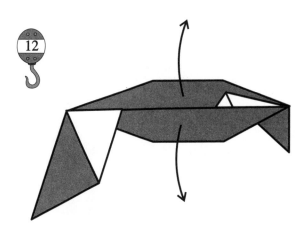

Open out the sides of the hull.

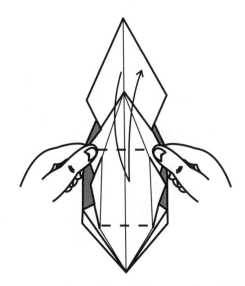

Grasp the sides of the hull and valley-fold between the corners and unfold. Repeat at the bottom.

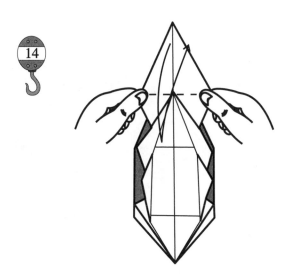

Grasp the sides of the sail; valley-fold and unfold. This will keep the sail open. Adjust the rudder to point downward.

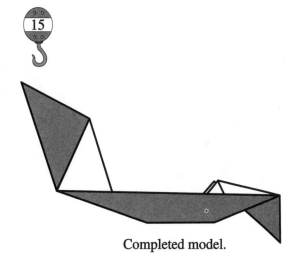

Completed model.

Short Raked-Stern Sailboat

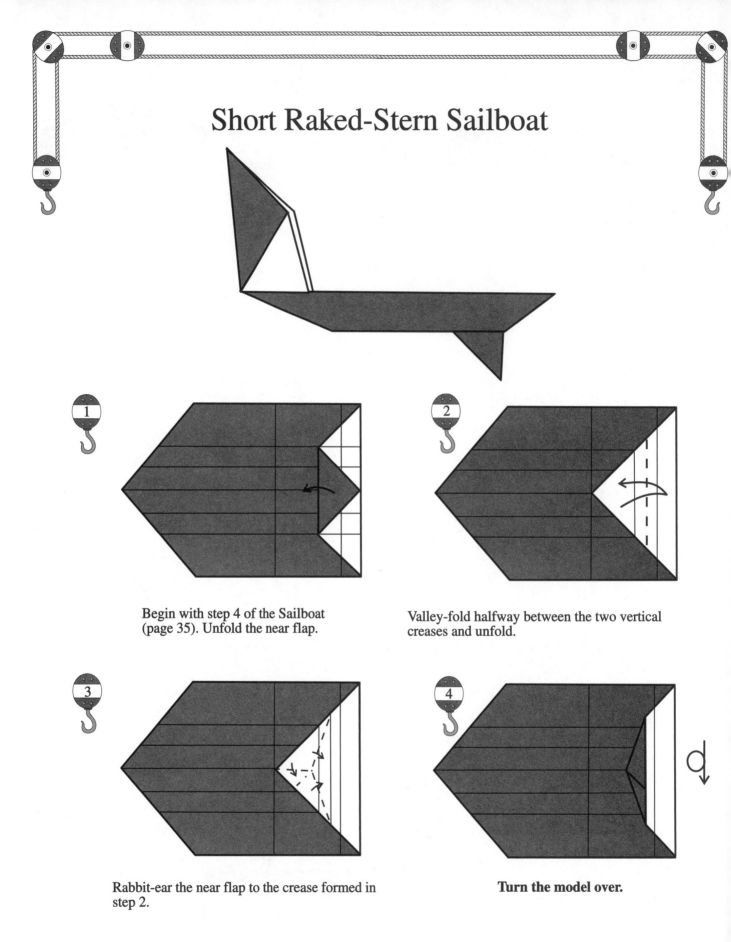

1

Begin with step 4 of the Sailboat (page 35). Unfold the near flap.

2

Valley-fold halfway between the two vertical creases and unfold.

3

Rabbit-ear the near flap to the crease formed in step 2.

4

Turn the model over.

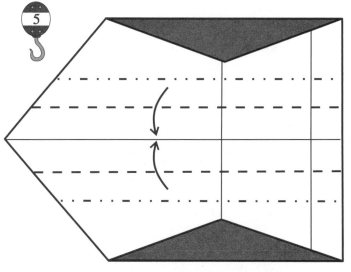

Enlarged view. Refold the valley and mountain folds so that the model looks like step 6.

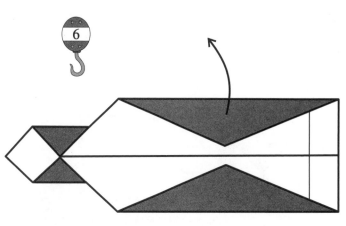

Open the near top flap completely.

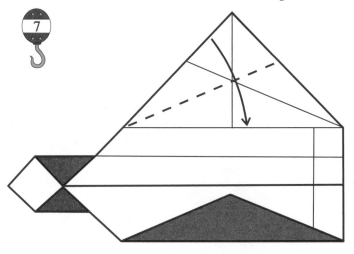

Valley-fold the upper left edge down along the existing crease.

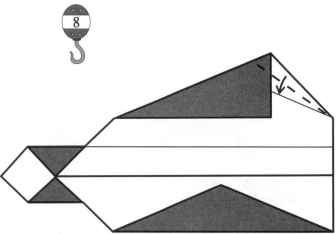

Valley-fold the upper right edge to the existing crease.

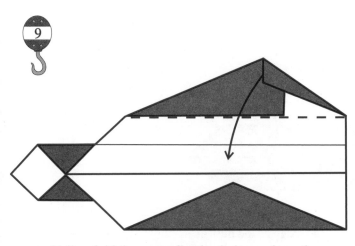

Valley-fold the upper flap back down along the existing horizontal crease.

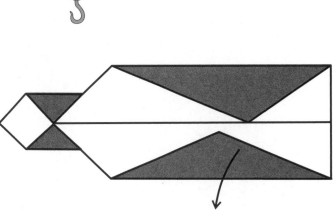

Repeat steps 6 through 9 on the lower flap.

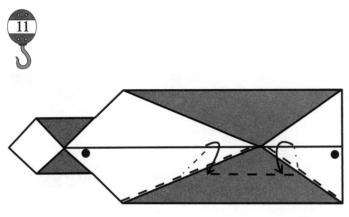

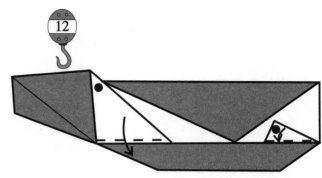

Boat-fold the bottom half. Watch the black dots.

Swing the left flap downward, opening the sail partway. Valley-fold the small triangular flap down into the hull. Then repeat step 11 above, boat-folding the upper half. Flatten the sail downward.

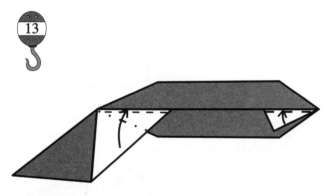

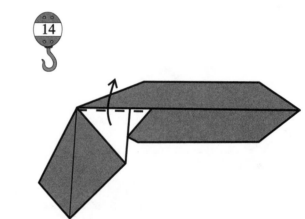

Swivel the near half of the sail up into the hull. Then valley-fold the small triangular flap up into the hull.

Lift the sail and repeat the swivel actions of step 13.

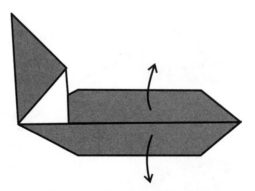

Open out the sides of the hull.

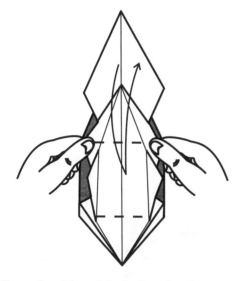

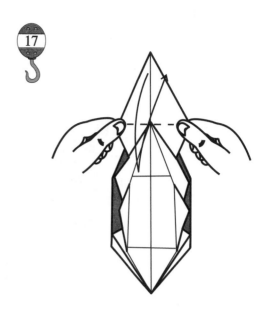

Grasp the sides of the hull and valley-fold between the corners and unfold. Repeat at the bottom.

Grasp the sides of the sail and valley-fold the model and unfold. This will keep the sail open. Adjust the rudder to point downward.

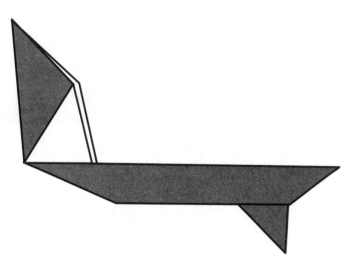

Side view of the completed Short Raked-Stern Sailboat.

Double-Ended Long Raked-Stern Sailboat

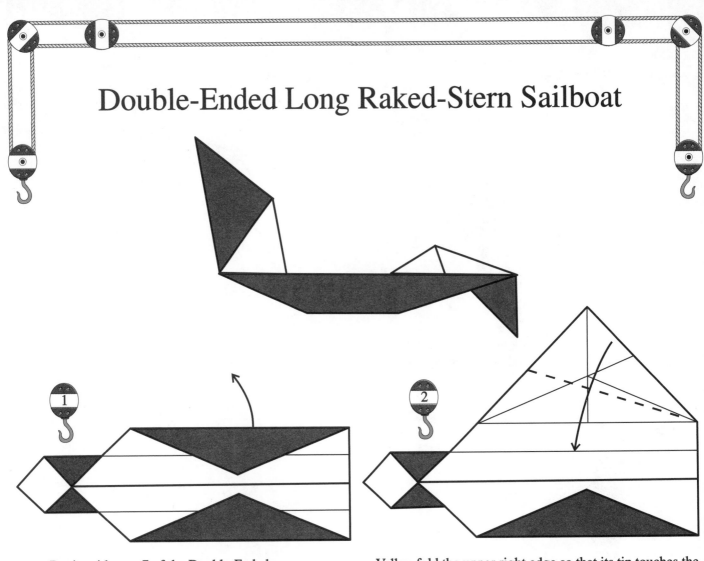

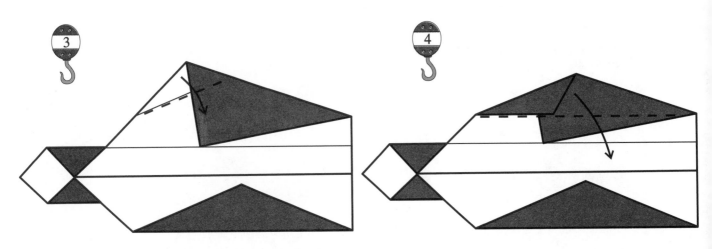

Begin with step 7 of the Double-Ended Sailboat (page 39). Open the near top flap completely.

Valley-fold the upper right edge so that its tip touches the horizontal crease nearest the centerline.

Valley-fold the top flap down along the existing crease.

Valley-fold the top flap downward; the crease is horizontal.

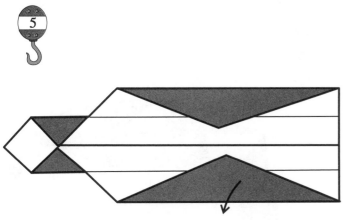

Repeat steps 1 through 4 on the lower near flap.

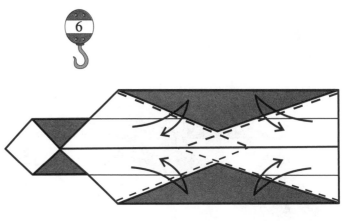

Valley-fold the upper and lower flaps along the folded edges and unfold.

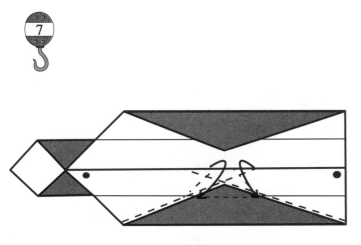

Boat-fold the lower half of the sailboat. The two folds will overlap in the middle. Watch the black dots.

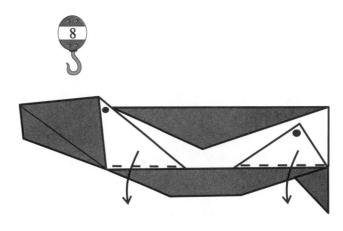

Swing the near left flap down, opening the sail partway. Swing the small triangular flap downward. Then repeat step 7, boat-folding the top half. Flatten the sail downward.

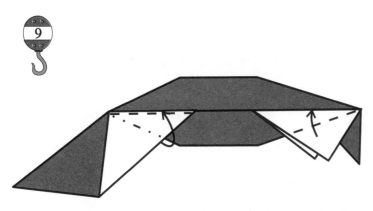

Swivel the near half of the sail up into the hull. Then valley-fold the near right flap up into the hull to form a coaming.

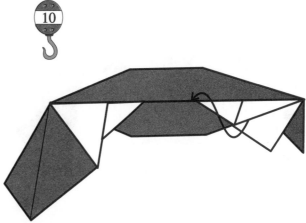

Tuck the finished coaming, still pointed downward, down into the lower half of the hull.

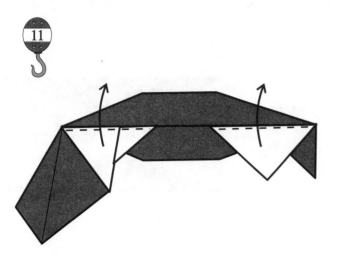

11

Swing the sail and the small triangular flap upward. Repeat the actions of step 9. Flatten the sail downward.

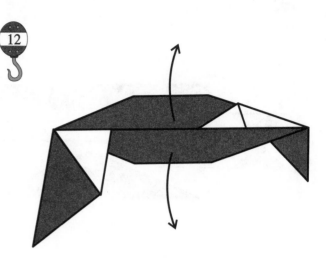

12

Open out the sides of the hull.

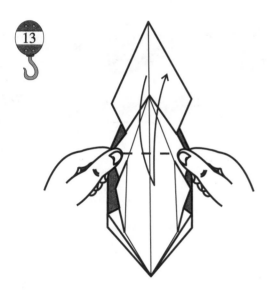

13

Grasp the sides of the hull and valley-fold between the corners and unfold. Repeat at the bottom.

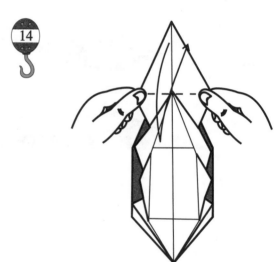

14

Grasp the sides of the sail, valley-fold and unfold. This will keep the sail open. Adjust the rudder to point downward.

15

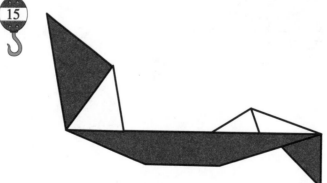

Side view of the Double-Ended Long Raked-Stern Sailboat.

Narrrow and Wide Sailboats

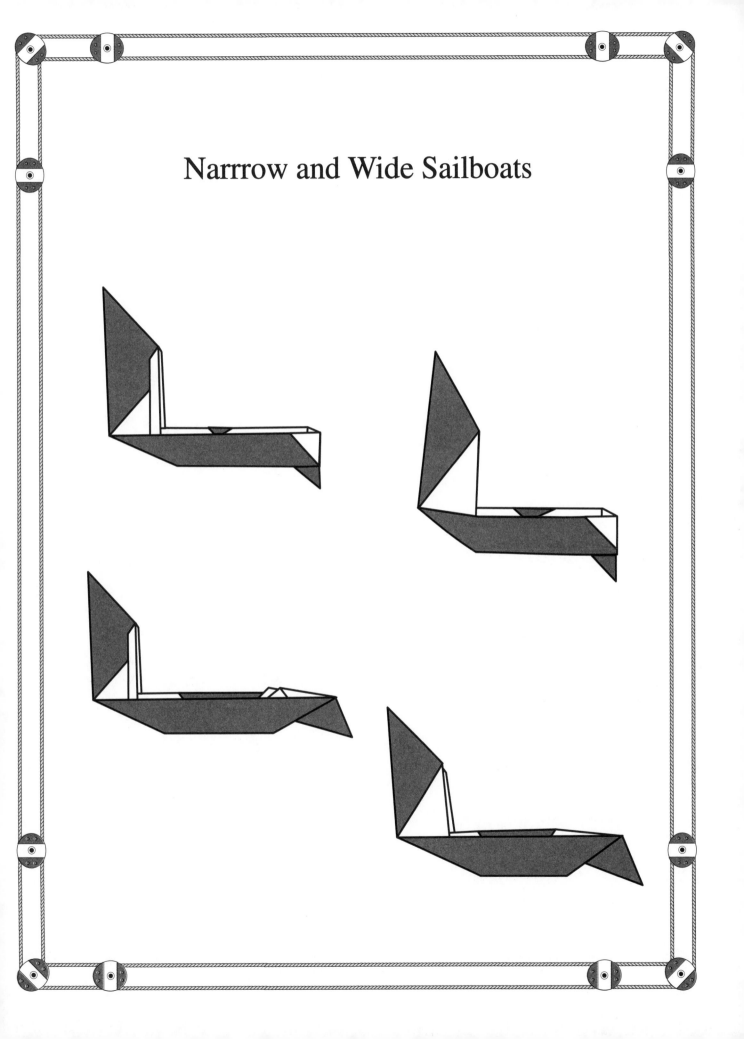

Narrow Sailboat

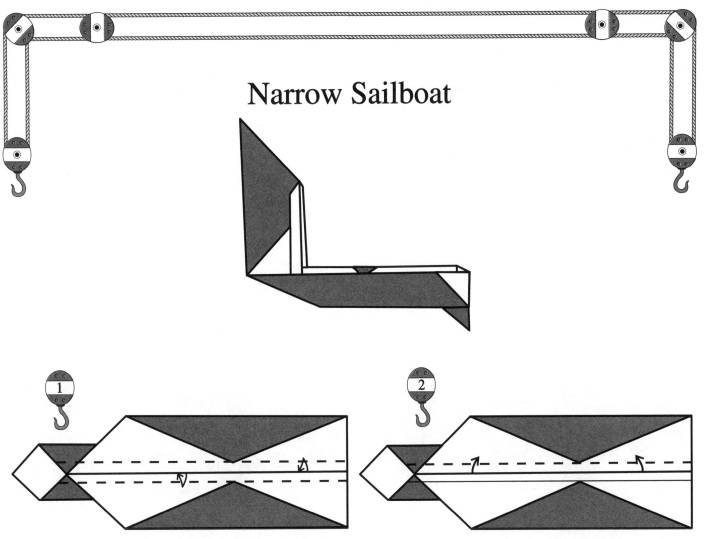

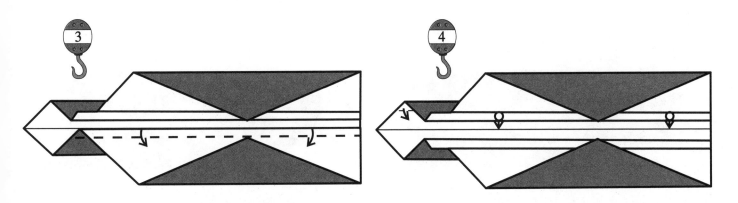

1 Begin with step 8 of the Sailboat (page 35). Valley-fold the upper half parallel to the centerline at the point of the near flap and unfold. Repeat below.

2 Valley-fold the upper inside edge along the crease formed in step 1 and tuck this edge under the near flap.

3 Repeat step 2 on the lower half of the model.

4 Grasp at the sides the folded cuff of the upper flap and slide the entire flap downward so that its lower edge lies along the centerline. Flatten the model.

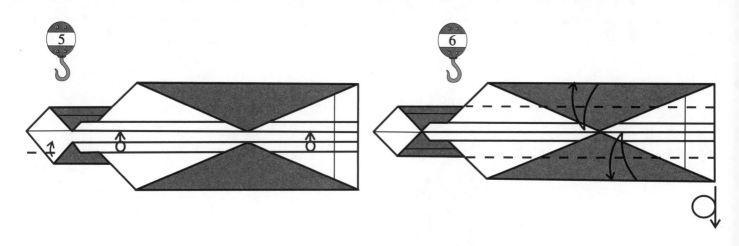

Repeat step 4 on the lower half.

Valley-fold the upper edge down to the centerline and unfold. Repeat below. **Turn the model over.**

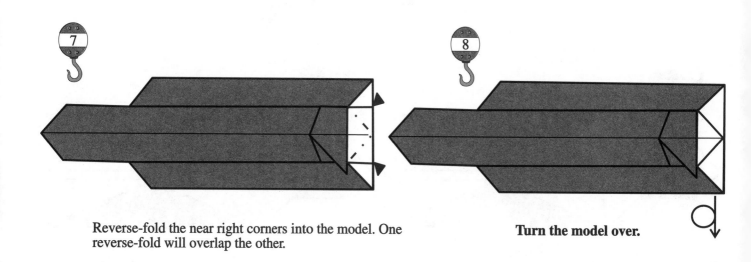

Reverse-fold the near right corners into the model. One reverse-fold will overlap the other.

Turn the model over.

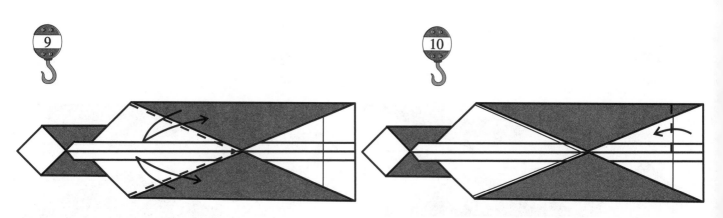

Valley-fold at the left along the folded edges and unfold.

Valley-fold the upper right edge leftward along the existing crease. A triangular collar will form itself.

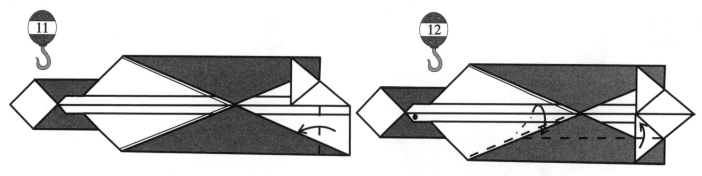

Valley-fold the lower right edge leftward along the existing crease. A triangular collar will form itself.

Boat-fold the lower left half, and valley-fold the lower edge upward to form the near side of the hull. Watch the black dot.

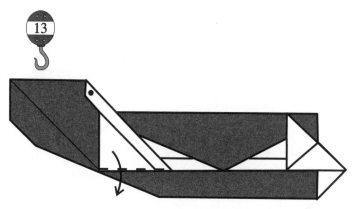

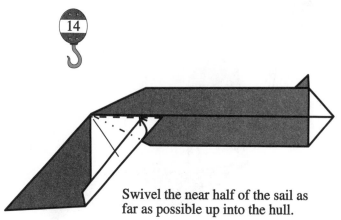

Swing the sail downward, opening it partway. Then repeat step 12 on the upper half. Flatten the sail downward.

Swivel the near half of the sail as far as possible up into the hull.

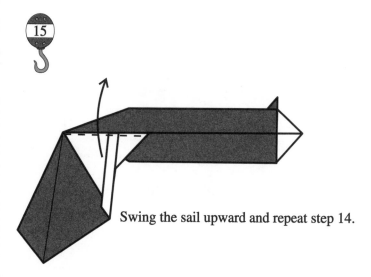

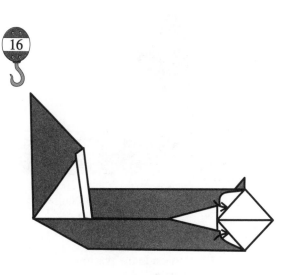

Swing the sail upward and repeat step 14.

Tuck the inner right corners into the triangular pockets behind them.

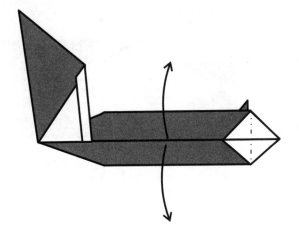

Open sides of the hull.
Square the transom.

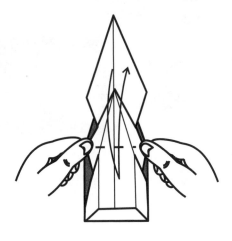

Grasp the sides of the hull and valley-fold between the corners and unfold. Adjust the rudder to point downward.

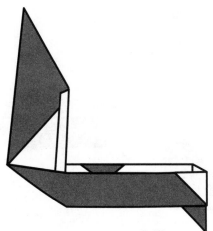

Side view of the Narrow Sailboat.

Top view of the Narrow Sailboat.

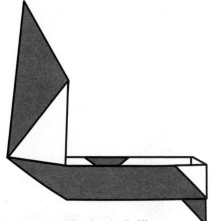

Side view of the basic Sailboat.

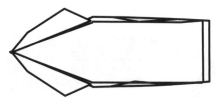

Top view of the basic Sailboat.

From the side the Narrow Sailboat appears identical to the Sailboat, but the Narrow Sailboat moves faster in the water.

Wide Sailboat

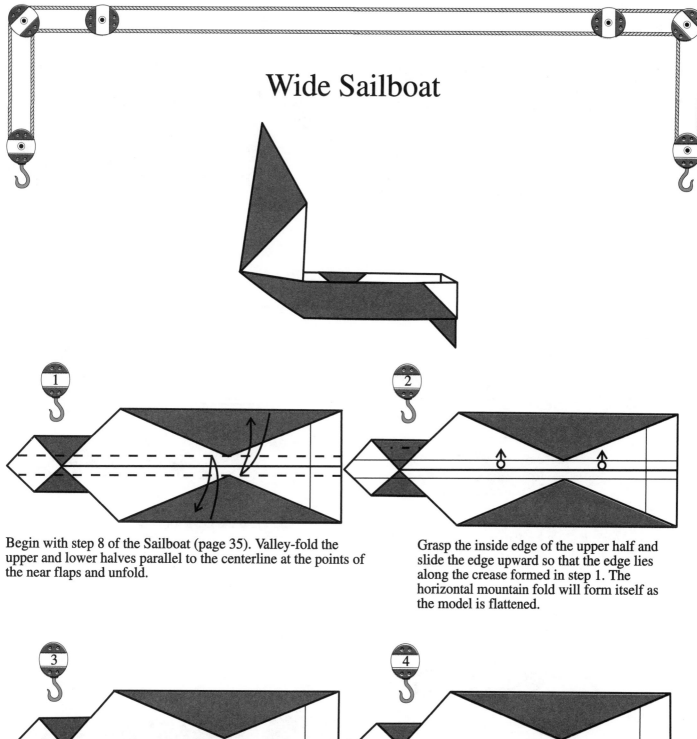

Begin with step 8 of the Sailboat (page 35). Valley-fold the upper and lower halves parallel to the centerline at the points of the near flaps and unfold.

2

Grasp the inside edge of the upper half and slide the edge upward so that the edge lies along the crease formed in step 1. The horizontal mountain fold will form itself as the model is flattened.

3

Repeat step 2 on the lower half.

4

Turn the model over.

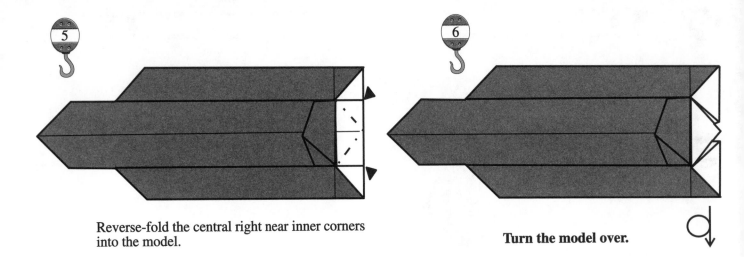

Reverse-fold the central right near inner corners into the model.

Turn the model over.

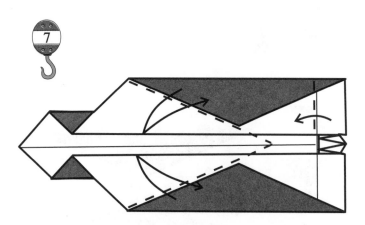

Valley-fold all layers at the left along the folded edges and unfold. Valley-fold the upper right edge leftward along the existing crease. A triangular collar will form itself as the model is flattened.

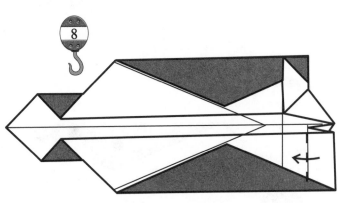

Valley-fold the lower right edge leftward along the existing crease. A triangular collar will form itself.

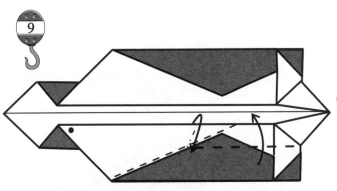
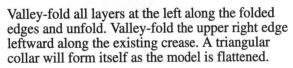

Boat-fold the lower left half. Valley-fold the lower edge of the bottom flap up to the centerline. Watch the black dot.

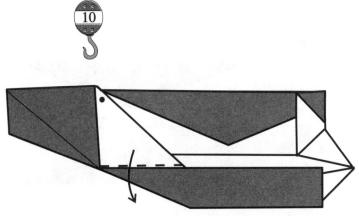

Swing the near half of the sail downward, opening it partway. Then repeat step 9 above. Flatten the sail downward.

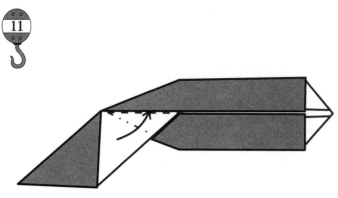

Swivel the near layers of the sail up into the hull.

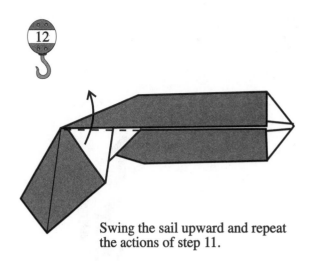

Swing the sail upward and repeat the actions of step 11.

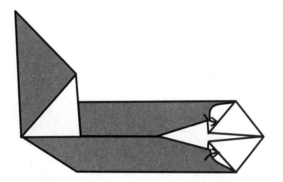

Tuck the inner right corners into the triangular pockets behind them.

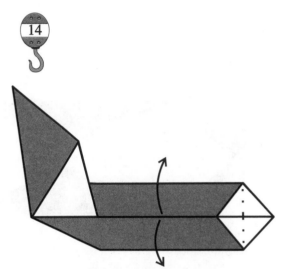

Open out the sides of the hull. Square the transom.

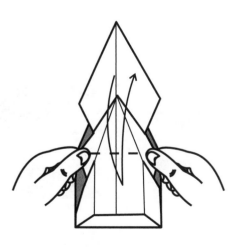

Grasp the sides of the hull and valley-fold between the corners and unfold. Adjust the rudder to point downward.

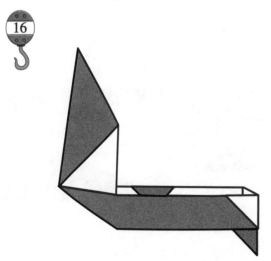

Side view of the Wide Sailboat.

Double-Ended Narrow Sailboat

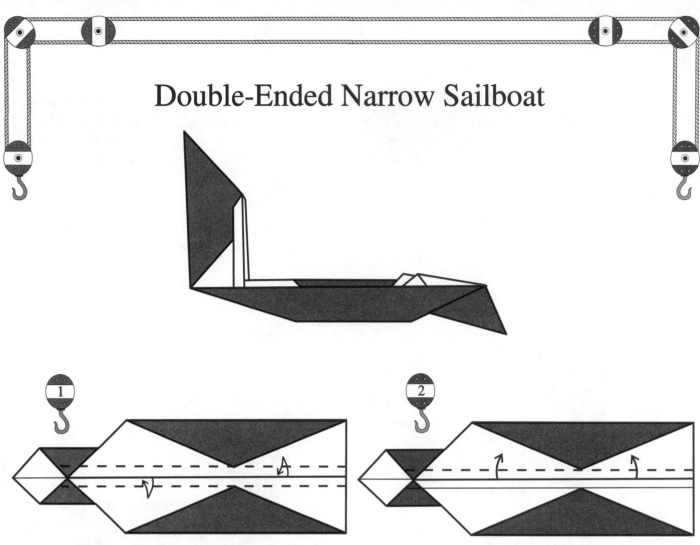

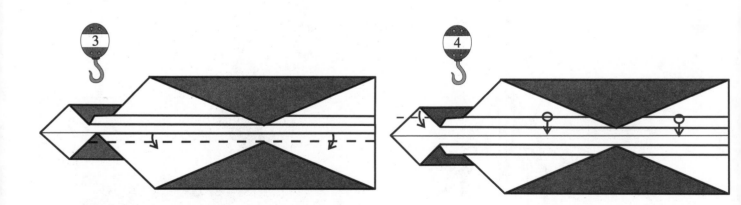

1

Begin with step 7 of the Double-Ended Sailboat (page 39).
Valley-fold the upper and lower halves parallel to the centerline
at the points of the near flaps and unfold.

2

Valley-fold the upper inside edge along the
crease formed in step 1 and tuck this edge under
the near flap.

3

Repeat step 2 on the lower half of the model.

4

Grasp at the circles the folded cuff of the upper flap
and slide the entire flap downward so that its lower
edge lies along the centerline. Flatten the model.

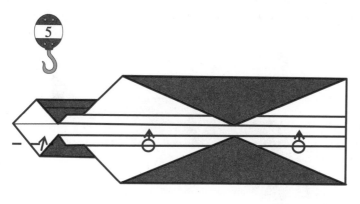

Repeat step 4 on the lower half.

Valley-fold the upper and lower edges of the model to the centerline and unfold.

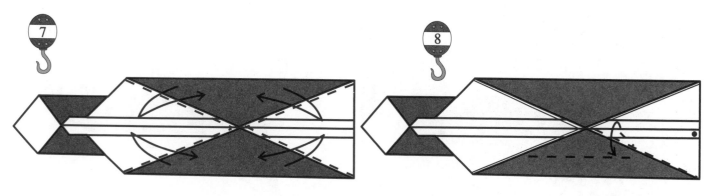

Valley-fold at the left along the folded edges and unfold. Repeat at the right.

Boat-fold the lower right half. Watch the black dot.

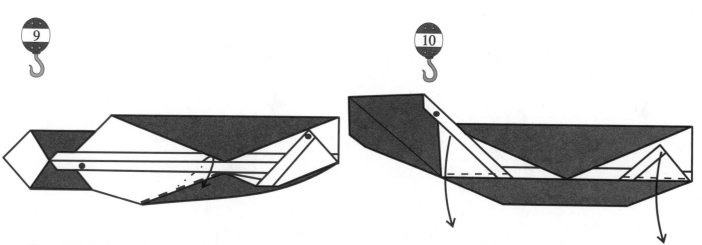

Boat-fold the lower left half. Watch the black dot.

Valley-fold the sail downward, opening it partway. Valley-fold the small triangular flap downward. Then repeat steps 8 and 9, boat-folding the upper half. Flatten the sail downward.

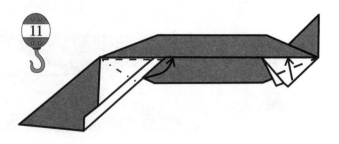

Swivel the near half of the sail up into the hull
and flatten. Valley-fold the near right flap up
into the hull as far as it will go.

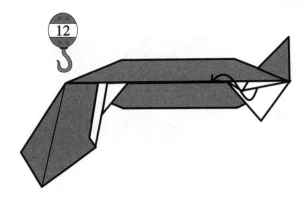

Tuck the finished coaming, still
pointed downward, down into the
lower half of the hull.

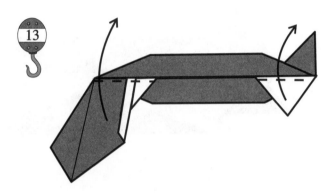

Swing the sail and the triangular
flap upward. Repeat the actions of
step 11. Flatten the sail downward.

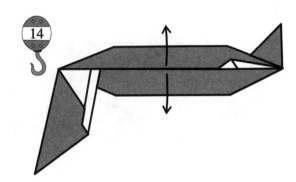

Open out the sides of the hull.

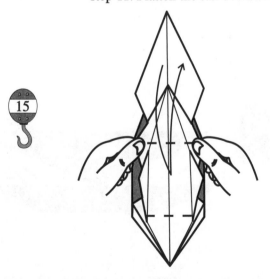

Grasp the sides of the hull and valley-fold
between the corners and unfold. Repeat at the
bottom. Adjust the rudder to point downward.

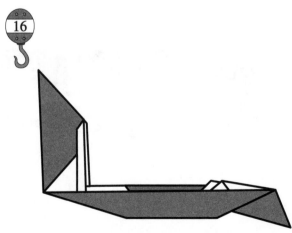

Side view of the Double-Ended Narrow Sailboat.

Double-Ended Wide Sailboat

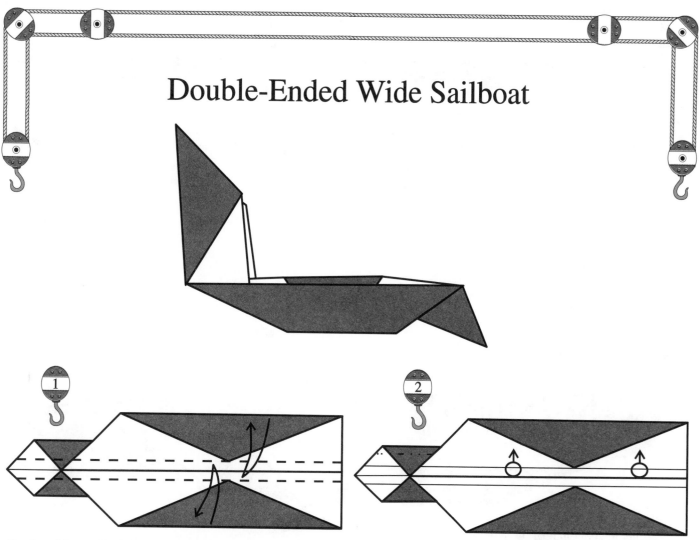

1

Begin with step 7 of the Double-Ended Sailboat (page 39).
Valley-fold the upper and lower halves parallel to the centerline
at the points of the near flaps and unfold.

2

Grasp the inside edge of the upper half and slide
the edge upward so that the edge lies along the
crease formed in step 1. The horizontal mountain
fold will form itself as the model is flattened.

3

Repeat step 2 on the lower half.

4

Valley-fold all the layers at the left along the folded
edges and unfold. Repeat at the right.

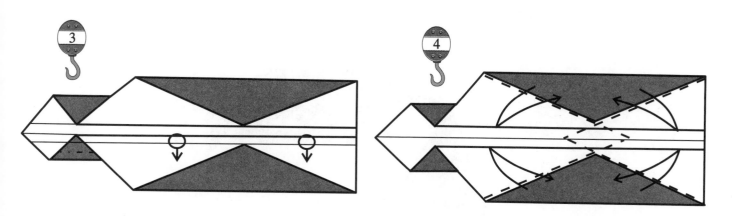

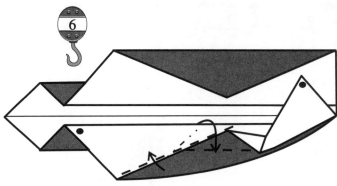

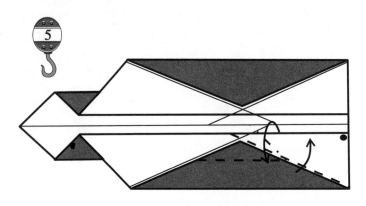

Boat-fold the lower right half of the model. Watch the black dot.

Boat-fold the lower left half. Watch the black dot.

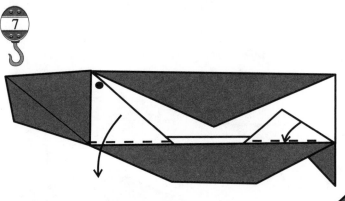

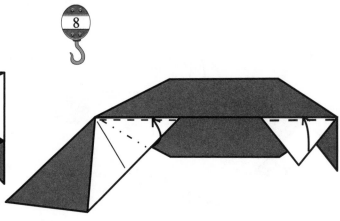

Swing the near half of the sail downward, opening it partway. Tuck the small triangular flap down into the hull. Then repeat steps 5 and 6 above. Flatten the sail downward.

Swivel the near half of the sail up into the hull as far as possible. Then tuck the near right flap up into the model.

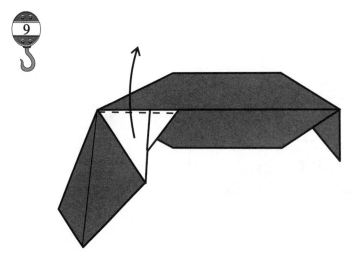

Swing the sail upward and repeat step 8. Flatten the sail downward.

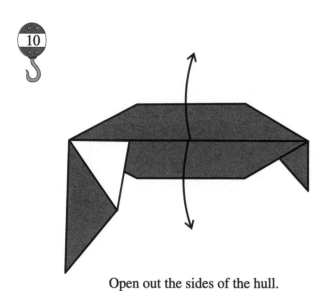

10

Open out the sides of the hull.

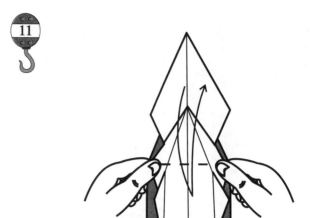

11

Grasp the sides of the hull and valley-fold between the corners and unfold. Repeat at the bottom.

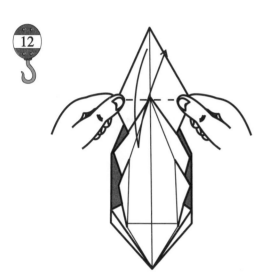

12

Grasp the sides of the sail and valley-fold and unfold. This will keep the sail open. Adjust the rudder to point downward.

13

Side view of the Double-Ended Wide Sailboat.

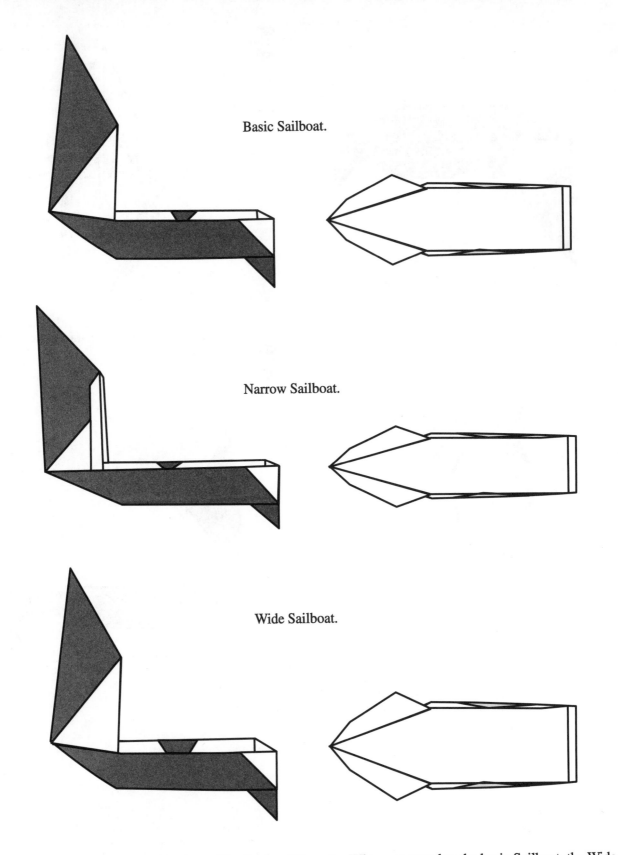

Basic Sailboat.

Narrow Sailboat.

Wide Sailboat.

Although the sailboats look similar they will sail very differently. When compared to the basic Sailboat, the Wide Sailboat will sail slowly and the Narrow Sailboat will move more swiftly through the water.

Sailboat Stabilizers

Stabilizers are large blocks of wood or metal that are lowered into the water from the bottom of the sailboat. These help to keep the sailboat from rocking from side to side while sailing.

Centerboard Stabilizers are single boards which are lowered from the center of the sailboat:

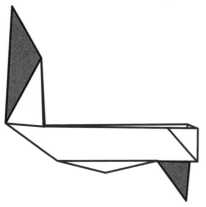 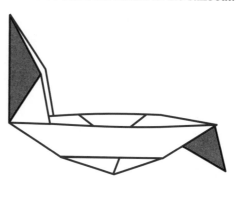

Bilge Board stabilizers are two boards which are attached to the sides of the sailboat (the Bilge area of the sailboat):

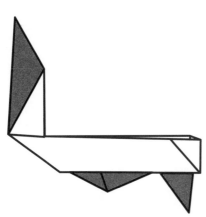 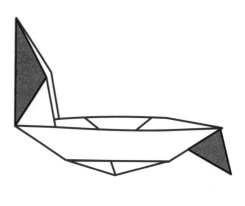

Leeboard stabilizers are usually found on Dutch sailboats; they are located on the outside of the hull:

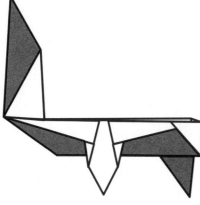 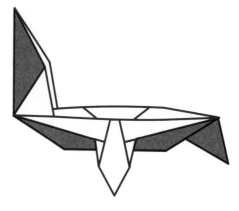

Centerboard Sailboat

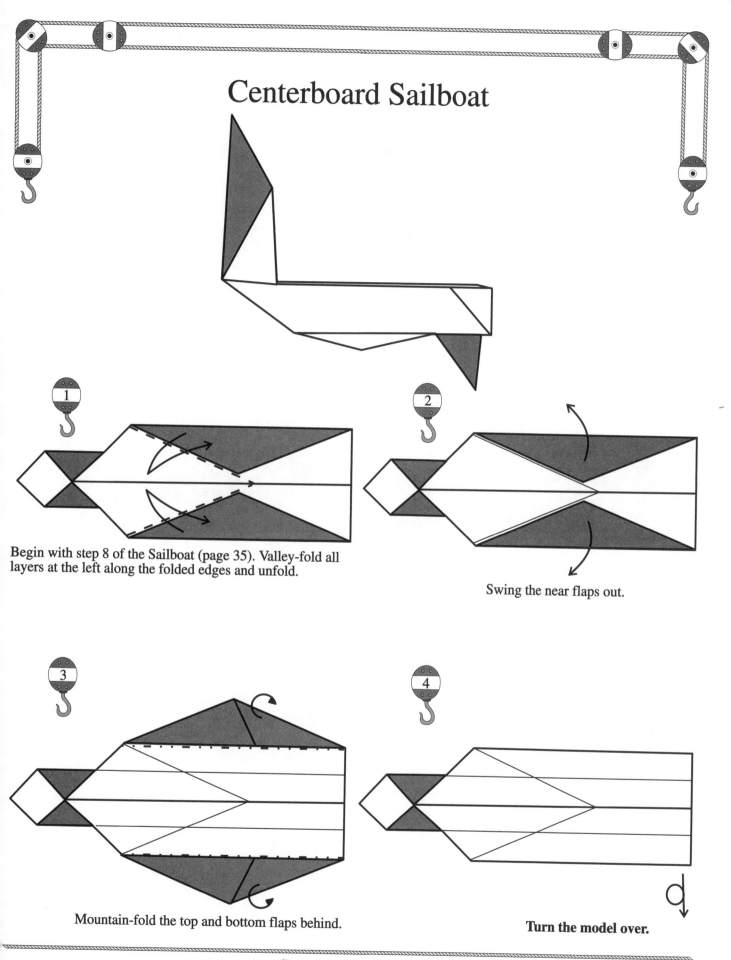

1 Begin with step 8 of the Sailboat (page 35). Valley-fold all layers at the left along the folded edges and unfold.

2 Swing the near flaps out.

3 Mountain-fold the top and bottom flaps behind.

4 **Turn the model over.**

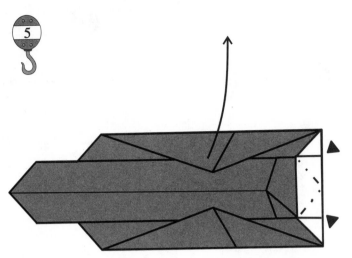

Enlarged view. Unfold the top near flap completely.
Reverse-fold the right near inner corners into the
model.

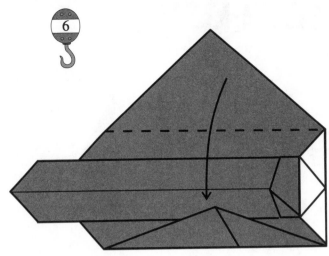

Valley-fold the top flap down as shown.

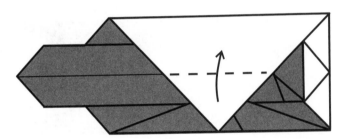

Valley-fold the near flap up along the centerline.

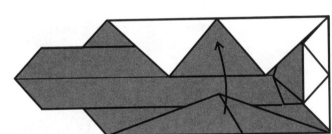

Open upward the near lower flap.

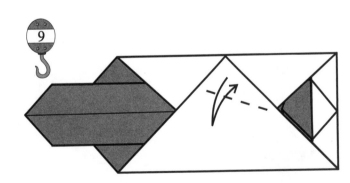

Valley-fold the right raw edge of the double flap
down so that it lies along the centerline and crease the
double flap. Unfold.

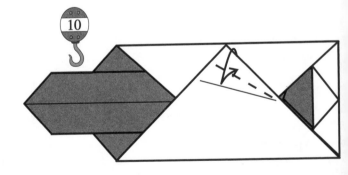

Valley-fold both upper right near edges down to
the crease formed in step 9 and unfold. Repeat
steps 9 and 10 on the upper left near edges.

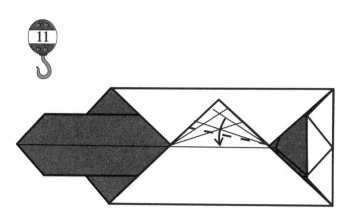

Valley-fold the upper right edges of the double flap so that the crease formed in step 10 lies along the centerline.

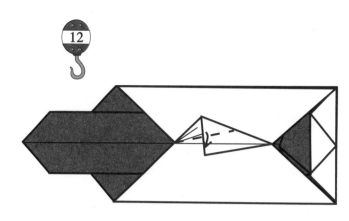

Valley-fold the upper left edge of the double flap so that the crease formed in step 10 lies along the centerline.

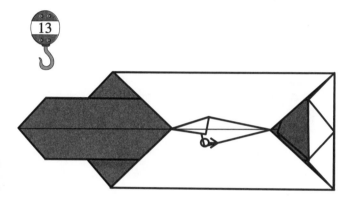

Pull out the small flap from inside the central construction, and flatten the flap to the right.

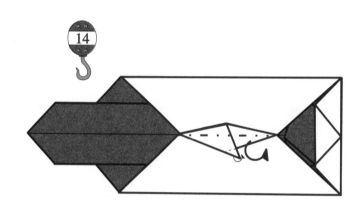

First tuck in the small triangular tip of the near flap; then mountain-fold the entire lower half of the central construction, tucking it up into the pocket formed by the upper half.

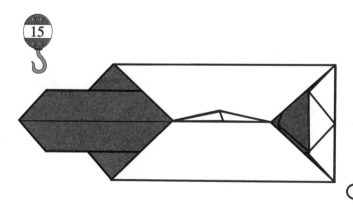

Turn the model over.

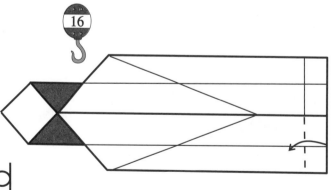

Valley-fold the bottom right edge leftward along the existing crease. A triangular collar will form itself.

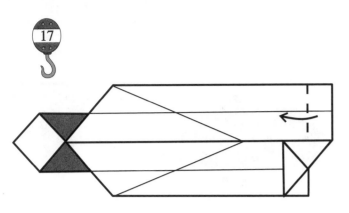

Repeat step 16 on the top right corner.

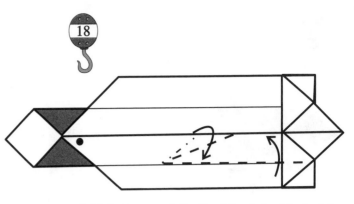

Boat-fold the bottom left side. Watch the black dot.

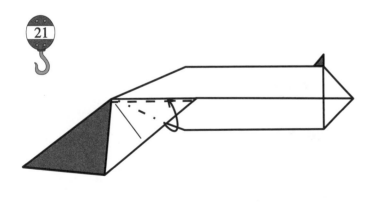

Reverse-fold the bottom left corner into the model.

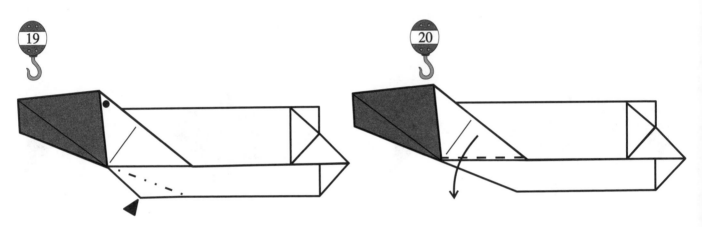

Swing the sail downward, opening it partway. Repeat steps 18 and 19 on the top half. Flatten the sail downward.

Swivel the near half of the sail up into the hull.

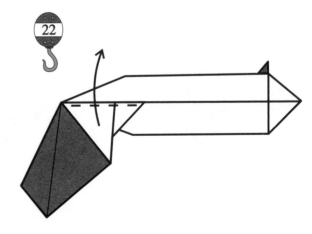

Swing the sail upward and repeat step 21. Flatten the sail downward.

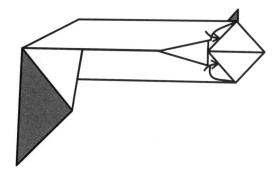

Tuck the inner right corners into the triangular pockets behind them.

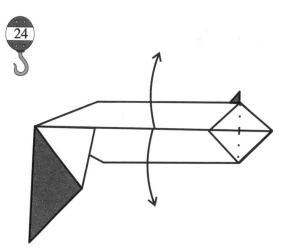

Open out the sides of the hull. Square the transom.

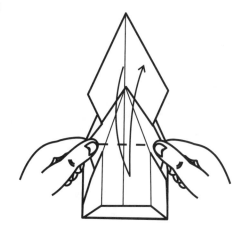

Grasp the sides of the hull and valley-fold between the corners and unfold.

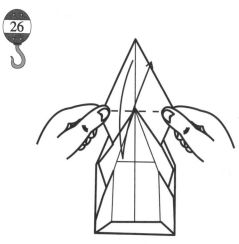

Grasp the sides of the sail and valley-fold and unfold. This will keep the sail open. Adjust the rudder to point downward.

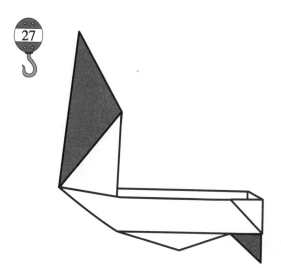

Side view of the Centerboard Sailboat.

Double-Ended Centerboard Sailboat

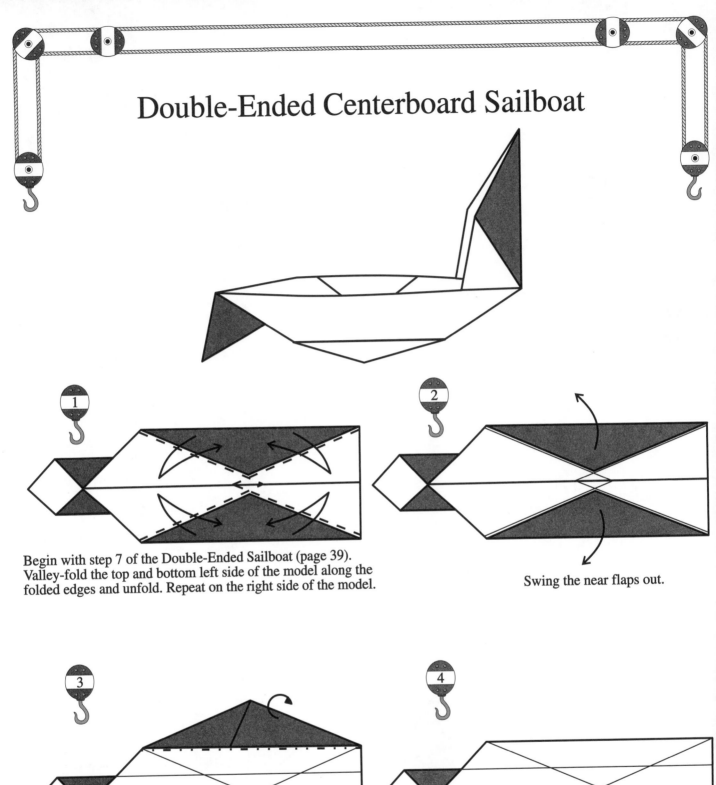

1

Begin with step 7 of the Double-Ended Sailboat (page 39). Valley-fold the top and bottom left side of the model along the folded edges and unfold. Repeat on the right side of the model.

2

Swing the near flaps out.

3

Mountain-fold the top and bottom flaps behind.

4

With the flaps still folded behind, fold the model as in steps 8 through 11 of the Double-Ended Sailboat (page 39).

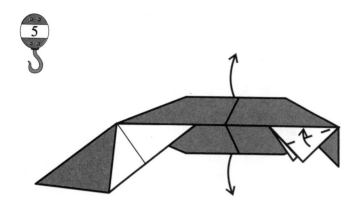

Bring the hidden flaps out from behind. Valley-fold the near triangular flap to the centerline.

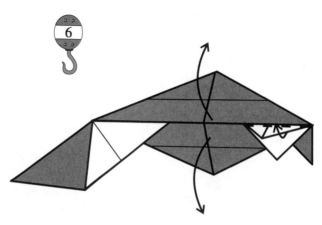

Open out the near central flaps at the top and bottom. Valley-fold the small near right flap up into the hull.

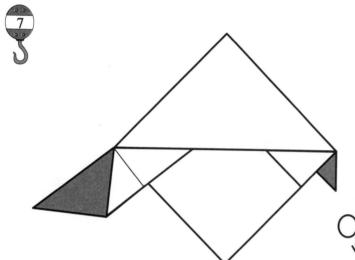

Turn the model over.

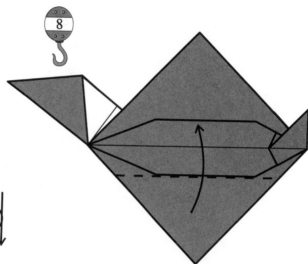

Valley-fold the bottom flap up along the folded edge.

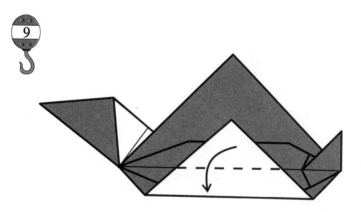

Valley-fold the near flap down along the centerline.

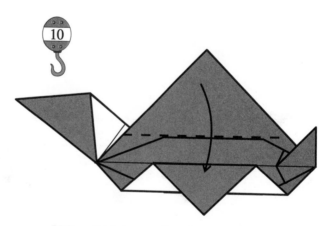

Valley-fold the top flap down along the folded edge of the hull.

Double-Ended Centerboard Sailboat 125

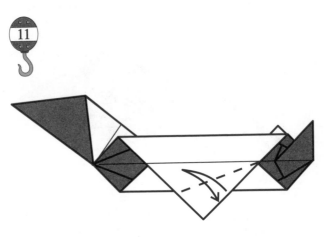

Valley-fold the right raw edges of the double flap up so that they lie along the centerline; then crease the double flap. Unfold.

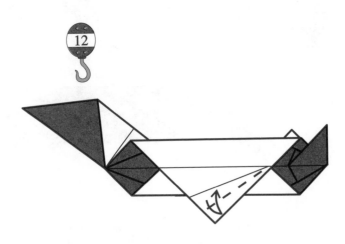

Valley-fold the the lower right near edges up to the crease formed in step 11 and unfold. Repeat steps 11 and 12 on the lower left near edges of the double flap.

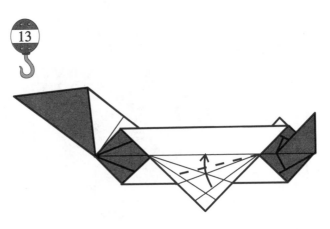

Valley-fold the lower right edges of the double flap so that the crease formed in step 12 lies along the centerline.

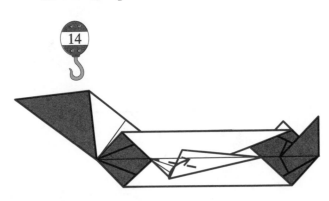

Valley-fold the lower left corner so that the crease formed in step 12 lies along the centerline.

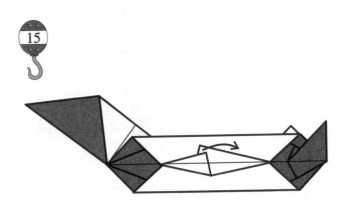

Pull out the small flap from inside the central construction and flatten the flap to the right.

First tuck in the small triangular tip of the near flap; then mountain-fold the entire upper half of the central construction, tucking it down into the pocket formed by the lower half.

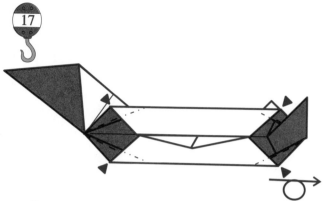

Reverse-fold the four corners of the near flaps inward between the two layers of paper forming the hull and **turn the model over** left to right.

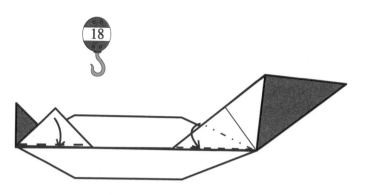

Swivel the near half of the sail down into the hull and flatten the sail downward. Then valley-fold the left flap downward.

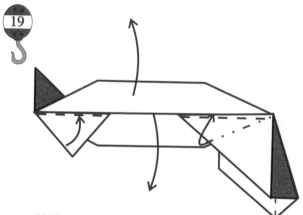

Valley-fold the near left flap, tucking it up into the hull. Swivel the near layers of the sail up into the hull. Then open out the sides of the hull.

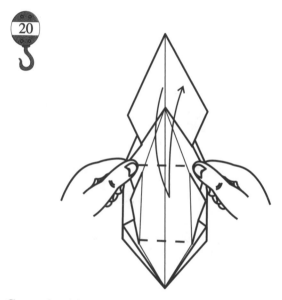

Grasp the sides of the hull and valley-fold between the corners and unfold. Repeat at the bottom.

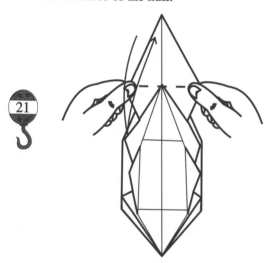

Grasp the sides of the sail and valley-fold and unfold. This will keep the sail open. Adjust the rudder to point downward.

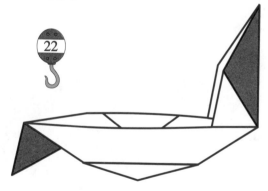

Point downward the small flap on the bottom of the sailboat. This forms the centerboard.

Bilge-Board Sailboat

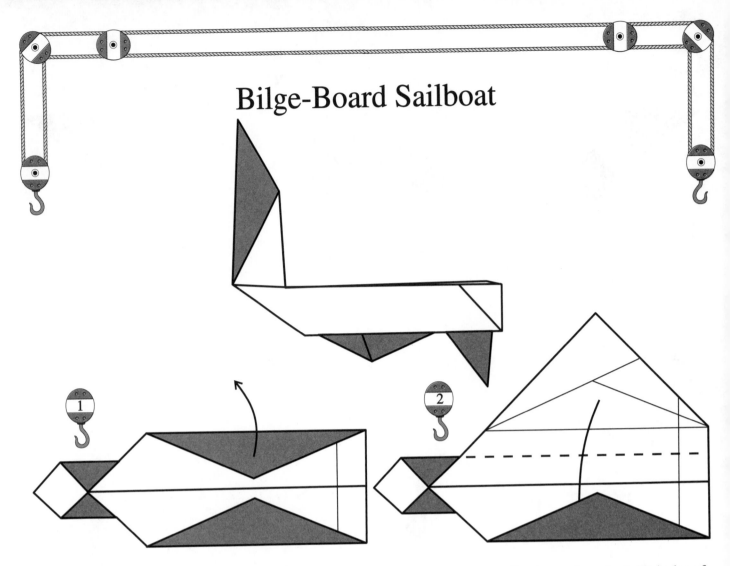

1 Begin with step 8 of the Sailboat (page 35). Open the near top flap completely.

2 Valley-fold the top flap down along the folded edge of the flap behind.

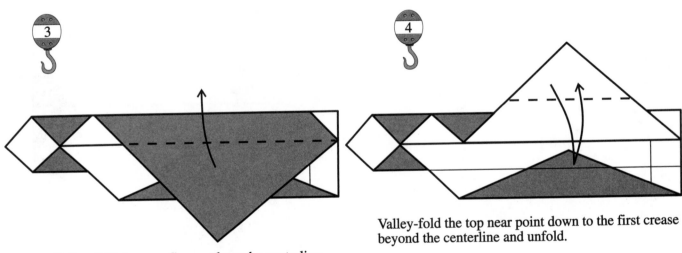

3 Valley-fold the near flap up along the centerline.

4 Valley-fold the top near point down to the first crease beyond the centerline and unfold.

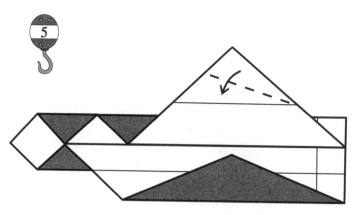

Valley-fold the top right edge down to the crease formed in step 4.

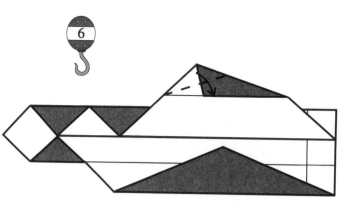

Valley-fold the top left edge down to the crease formed in step 4.

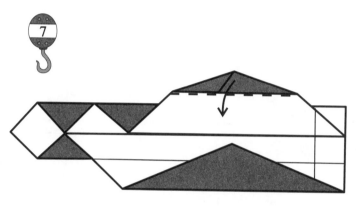

Valley-fold the top near flap down along the crease formed in step 4.

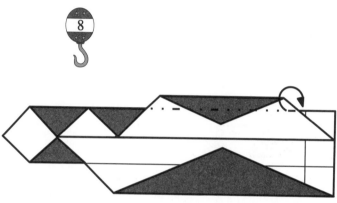

Mountain-fold the top near flap back over the single folded edge just behind it—the flap will lie in the back groove.

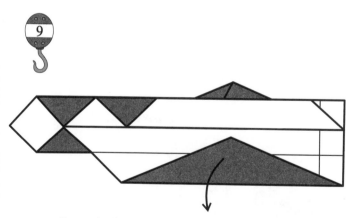

Open the bottom near flap completely. Repeat steps 1 through 8 on the bottom.

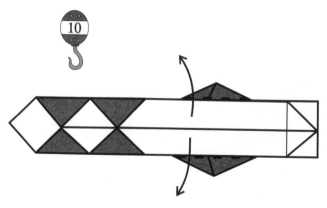

Swing only the two nearest flaps outward in a hinge action. The visible parts of both bilge boards remain vertical and do not move, and thus each board will automatically be valley-folded during the hinge movement.

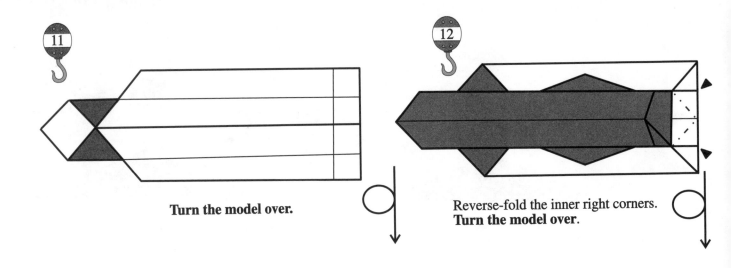

Turn the model over.

Reverse-fold the inner right corners.
Turn the model over.

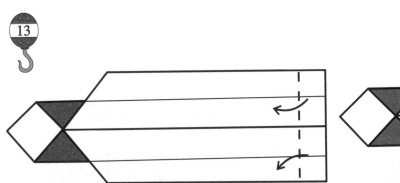

Valley-fold the right edge leftward along the existing crease, at both top and bottom.

Boat-fold the bottom left side. Watch the black dot.

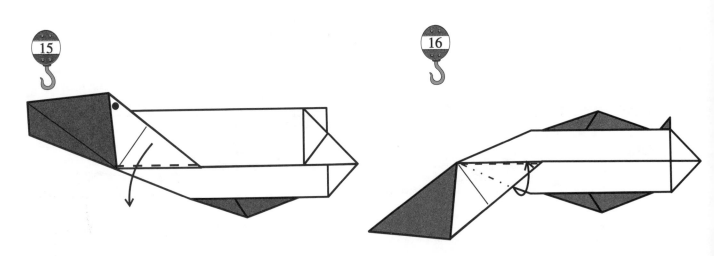

Swing the near half of the sail downward, opening it partway. Repeat step 14 on the upper half. Flatten the sail downward.

Swivel the near half of the sail up into the hull.

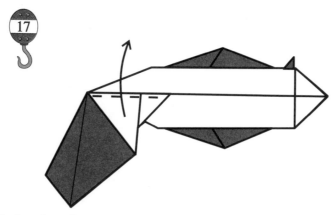

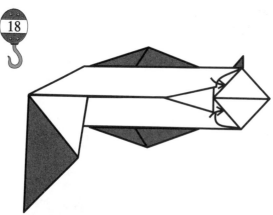

Swing the sail upward and repeat step 16. Flatten the sail downward.

Tuck the inner right corners into the triangular pockets behind them.

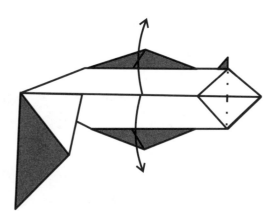

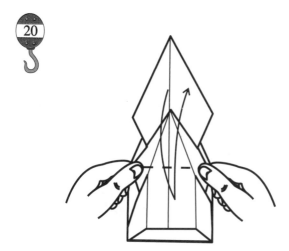

Open out the sides of the hull. Square the transom.

Grasp the sides of the hull and valley-fold between the corners and unfold.

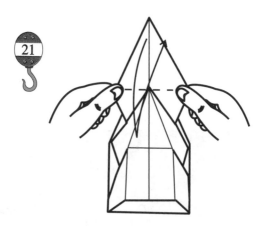

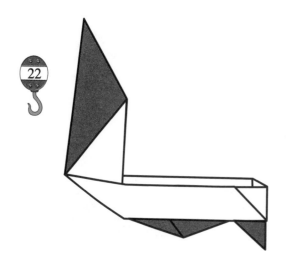

Grasp the sides of the sail. Valley-fold and unfold. This will keep the sail open. Adjust the rudder to point downward.

Side view of the Bilge-Board Sailboat.

Double-Ended Bilge-Board Sailboat

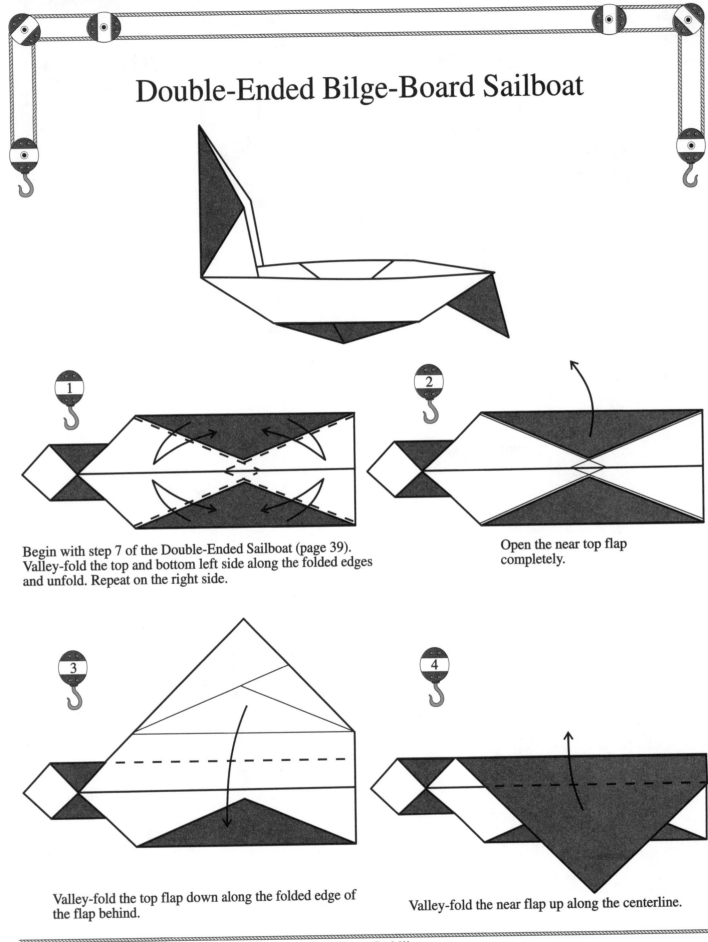

1

Begin with step 7 of the Double-Ended Sailboat (page 39).
Valley-fold the top and bottom left side along the folded edges
and unfold. Repeat on the right side.

2

Open the near top flap
completely.

3

Valley-fold the top flap down along the folded edge of
the flap behind.

4

Valley-fold the near flap up along the centerline.

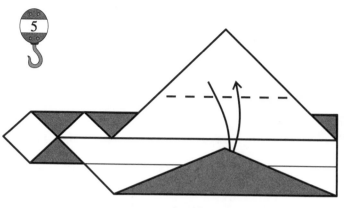

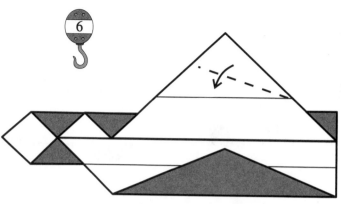

Valley-fold the top near point down to the first crease beyond the centerline and unfold.

Valley-fold the top right edge down to the crease formed in step 5.

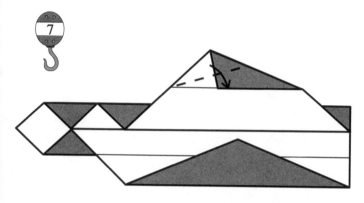

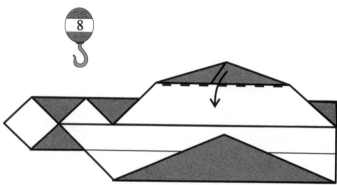

Valley-fold the top left edge down to the crease formed in step 5.

Valley-fold the top near flap down along the crease formed in step 5.

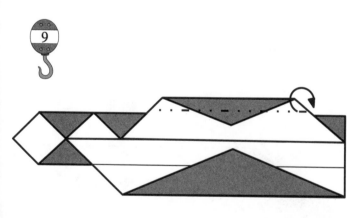

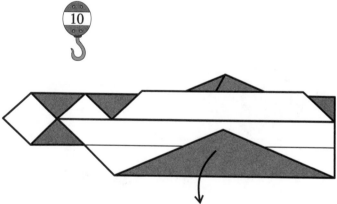

Mountain-fold the top near flap back over the single folded edge just behind it—the flap will lie in the back groove.

Unfold the bottom near flap completely. Repeat steps 3 through 9 on the bottom flap.

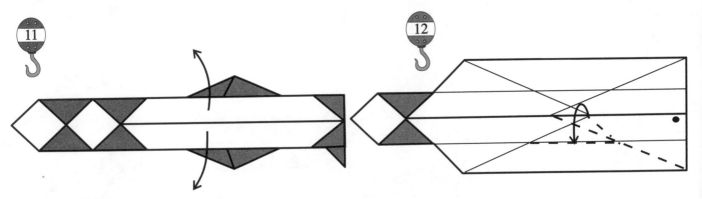

11

Swing only the front layer of the two nearest flaps outward in a hinge action. The visible parts of both bilge boards remain vertical and do not move.

12

Boat-fold the lower right side. Watch the black dot.

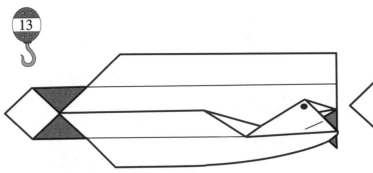

13

Step 13 shows this procedure in progress. Watch the black dot.

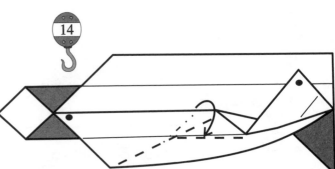

14

Boat-fold the bottom left side. Watch the black dot.

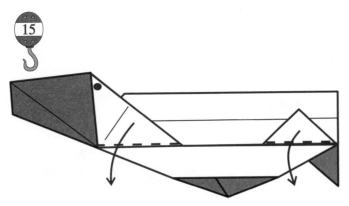

15

Swing the near half of the sail downward, opening it partway. Swing the right triangular flap downward. Repeat steps 12 through 14 on the top half. Flatten the sail downward.

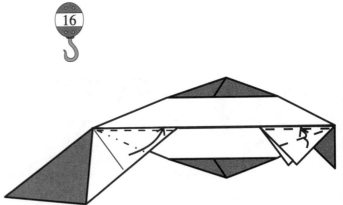

16

Swivel the near half of the sail up into the hull. Valley-fold the near right flap, tucking it up into the model.

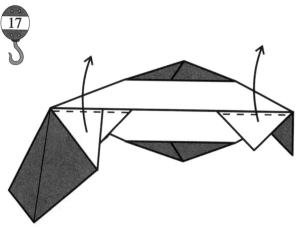

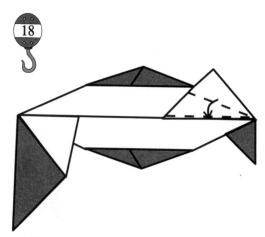

Swing the sail upward and repeat step 16. Flatten the sail downward. Then swing the small triangular flap upward.

Tuck the triangular flap down into the hull. The flaps on the top and bottom will form bilge-boards.

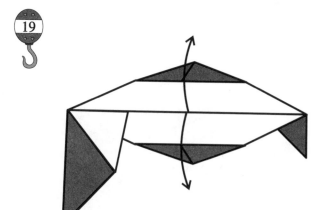

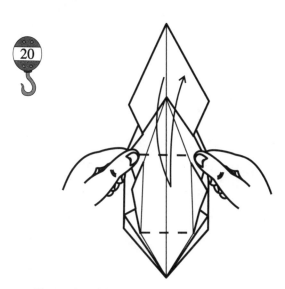

Open out the sides of the hull.

Grasp the sides of the hull and valley-fold between the corners and unfold. Repeat at the bottom.

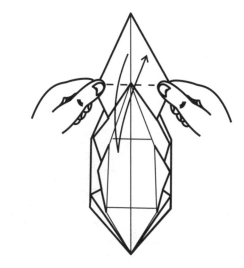

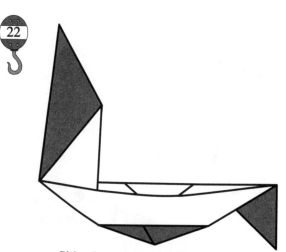

Grasp the sides of the sail, valley-fold and unfold. This will keep the sail open. Adjust the rudder to point downward.

Side view of the Double-Ended Bilge-Board Sailboat.

Leeboard Sailboat

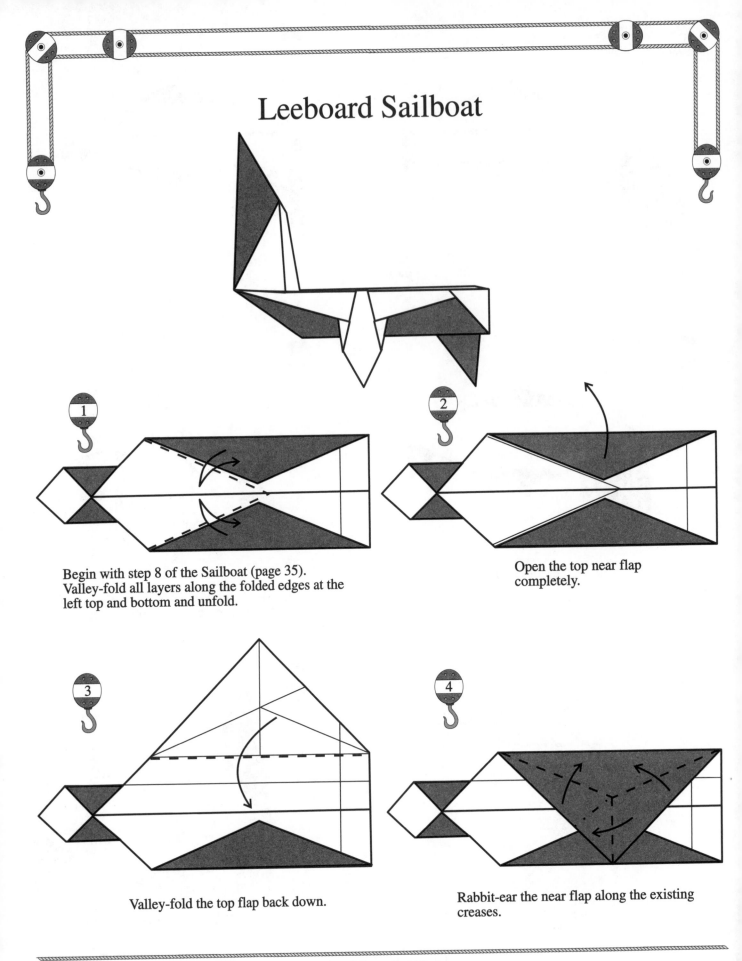

Begin with step 8 of the Sailboat (page 35). Valley-fold all layers along the folded edges at the left top and bottom and unfold.

Open the top near flap completely.

Valley-fold the top flap back down.

Rabbit-ear the near flap along the existing creases.

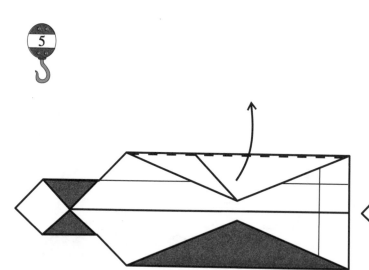

Swing the top flap upward in a hinge action.

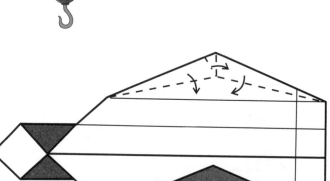

Rabbit-ear the top flap.

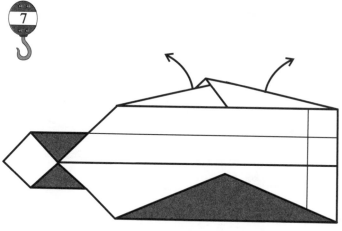

Bring the raw edges of the top flap out from behind.

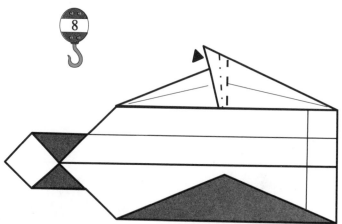

Lift and squash-fold the near flap by opening
it and flattening the flap symmetrically to the
left and right.

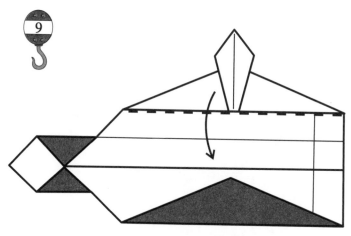

Valley-fold the top flap down.

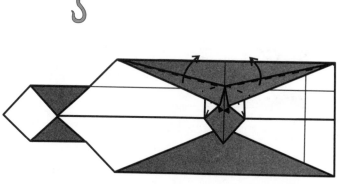

Valley-fold the raw edges of the near flap upward along
the folded edge. At the the same time squash-fold the
small inner corners into the triangular collars shown in
step 11.

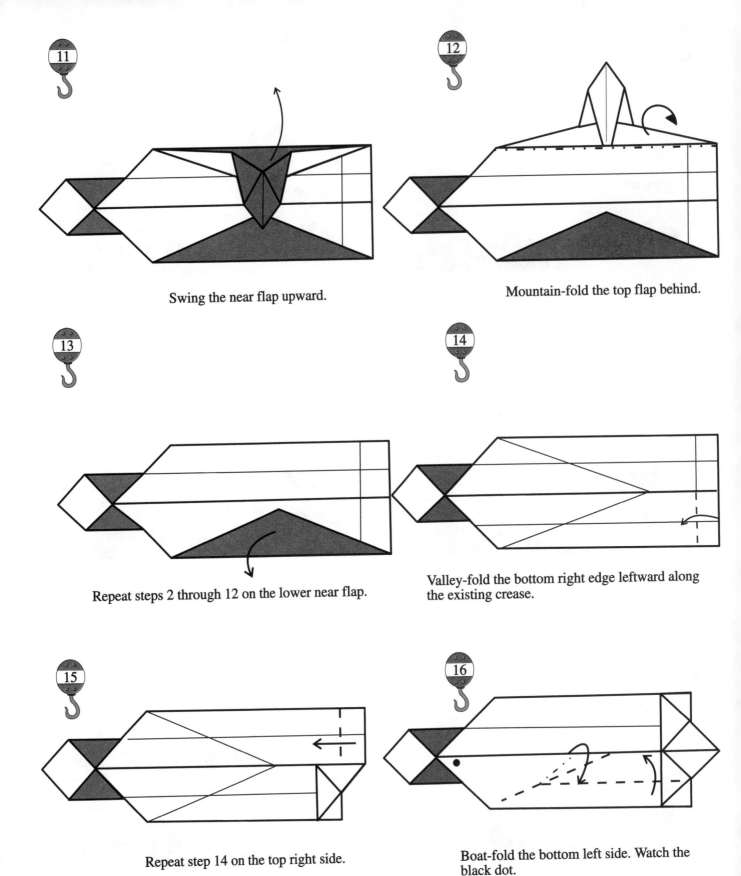

11

Swing the near flap upward.

12

Mountain-fold the top flap behind.

13

Repeat steps 2 through 12 on the lower near flap.

14

Valley-fold the bottom right edge leftward along the existing crease.

15

Repeat step 14 on the top right side.

16

Boat-fold the bottom left side. Watch the black dot.

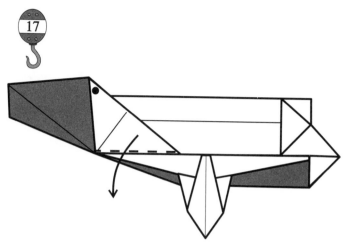

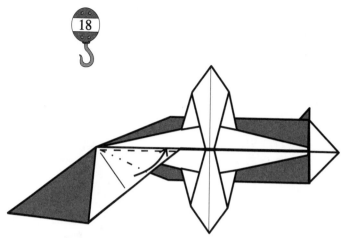

Swing the sail downward, opening it partway. Repeat step 16 on the top half. Flatten the sail downward.

Swivel the near half of the sail up into the hull.

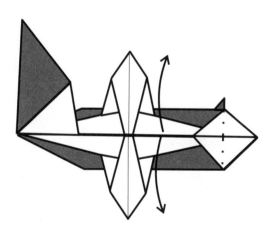

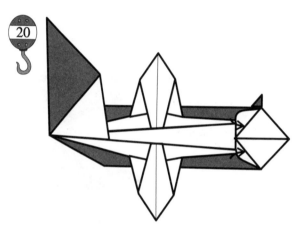

Swing the sail upward and repeat step 18.

Tuck the inner right corners into the triangular pockets behind them.

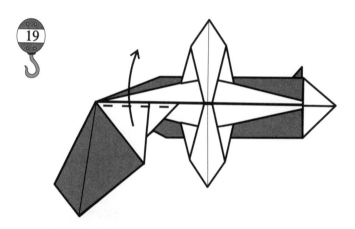

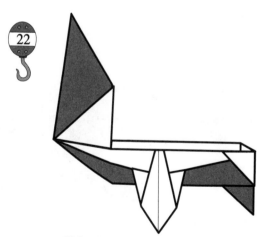

Open out the sides of the hull. Square the transom. Adjust the

Side view of the Leeboard Sailboat.

Double-Ended Leeboard Sailboat

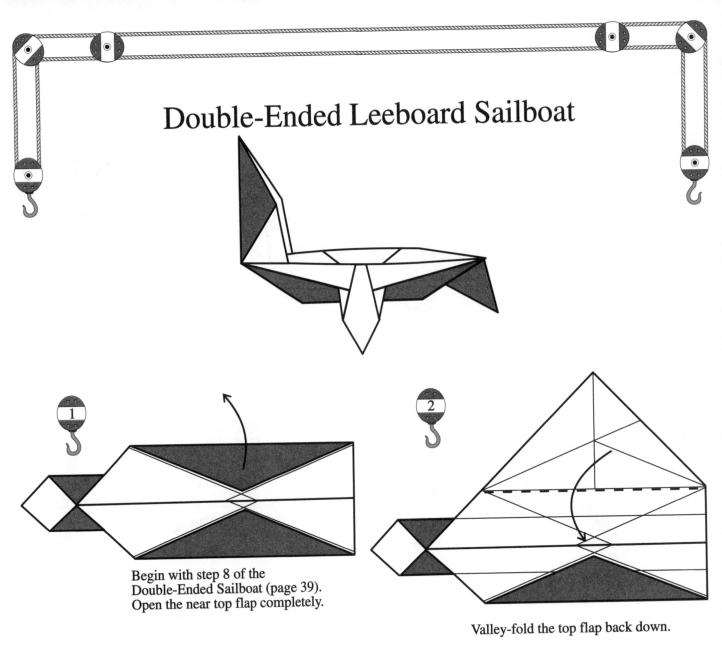

1 Begin with step 8 of the
Double-Ended Sailboat (page 39).
Open the near top flap completely.

2 Valley-fold the top flap back down.

3 Rabbit-ear the flap along the existing creases.

4 Swing the top flap upward in a hinge action.

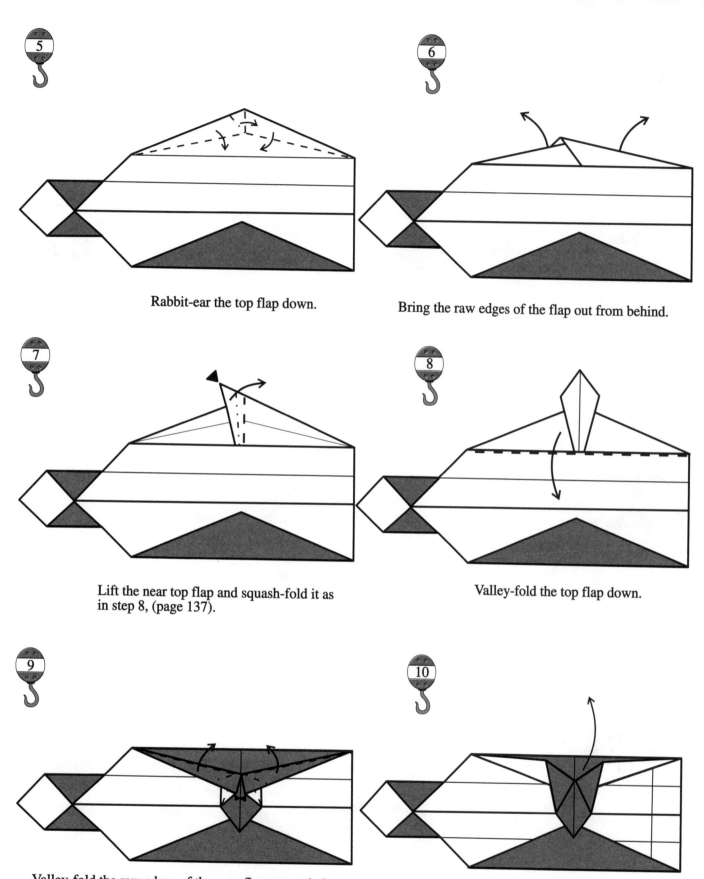

5

Rabbit-ear the top flap down.

6

Bring the raw edges of the flap out from behind.

7

Lift the near top flap and squash-fold it as in step 8, (page 137).

8

Valley-fold the top flap down.

9

Valley-fold the raw edges of the near flap upward along the folded edge. At the same time squash-fold the small inner corners into the triangular collars shown in step 10.

10

Swing the near flap upward in a hinge action.

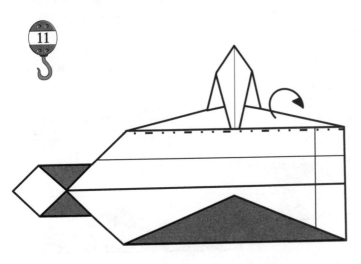

Mountain-fold the upper flap behind.

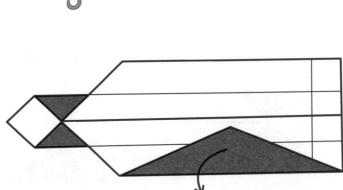

Repeat steps 1 through 11 on the lower near flap.

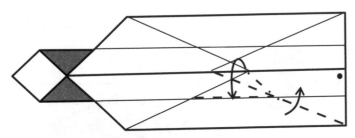

Boat-fold the lower right side. Watch the black dot.

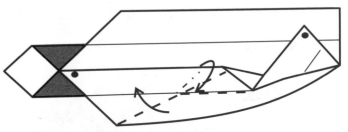

Boat-fold the bottom left side of the model. Watch the black dot.

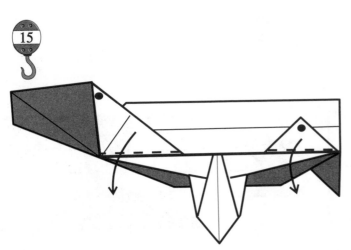

Swing the sail downward, opening it partway. Swing the small right flap downward. Repeat steps 13 and 14 on the top half. Flatten the sail downward.

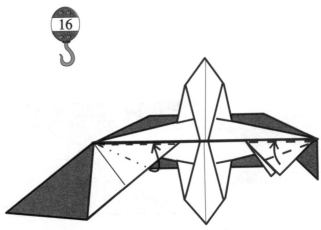

Swivel the near half of the sail up into the hull. Valley-fold the near right flap up to the centerline and then tuck it up into the hull.

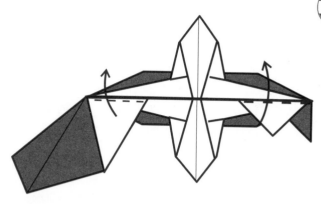

Swing the sail upward and repeat step 16. Swing the triangular flap upward. Flatten the sail downward.

Valley-fold the triangular flap in half and then tuck it down into the hull.

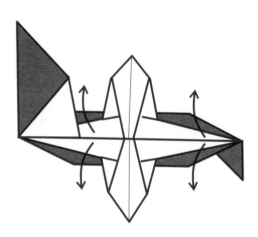

Open out the hull.

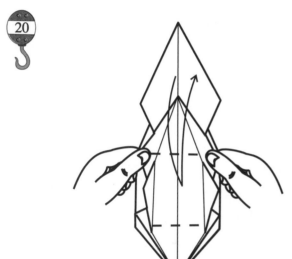

Grasp the sides of the hull and valley-fold between the corners and unfold. Repeat at the bottom.

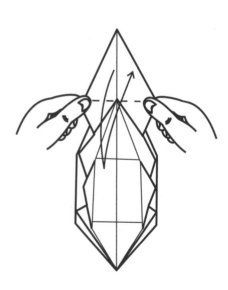

Grasp the sides of the sail and valley-fold and unfold. This will keep the sail open. Adjust the rudder to point downward.

The leeboards remain on the near and far sides of the sailboat.

Sailboat Design

Sailboat Designs

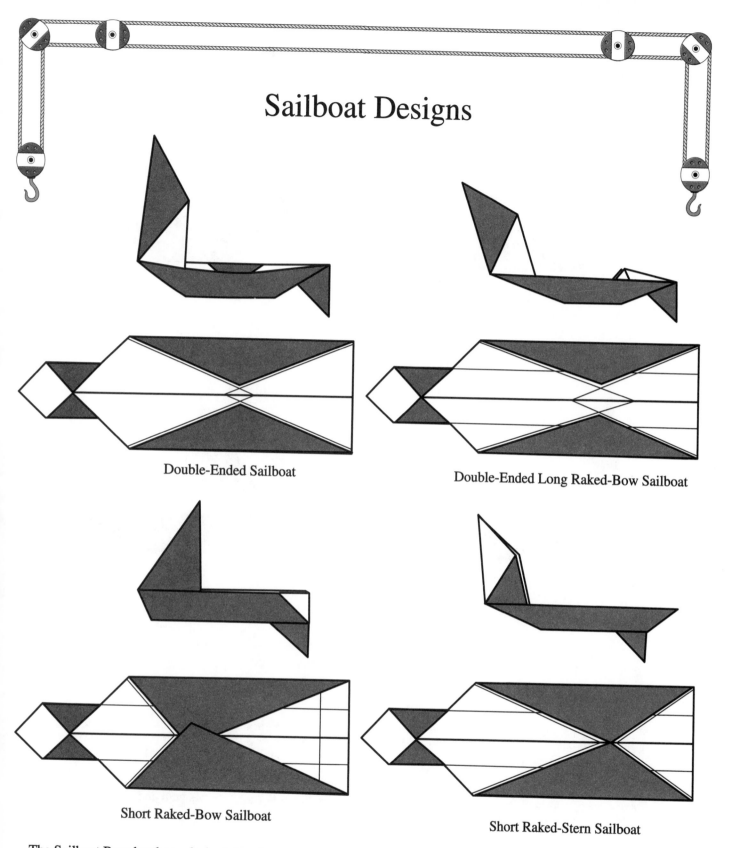

Double-Ended Sailboat

Double-Ended Long Raked-Bow Sailboat

Short Raked-Bow Sailboat

Short Raked-Stern Sailboat

The Sailboat Base has been designed so that you can change the bow and stern by increasing or decreasing the angle of the two near flaps. The top and bottom flaps can be opened to fold stabilizers or the stabilizers may be omitted. By choosing different hull configurations, you can design your own sailboats. Double-ended sailboats offer the greatest number of different combinations since both the bow and stern can be folded at different angles.

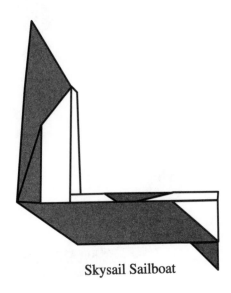

Skysail Sailboat

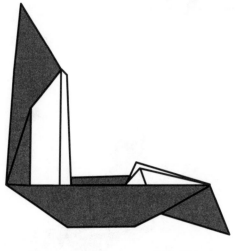

Double-Ended Skysail Sailboat

You can fold the sailboat hulls with a transom (the flat square end
of a sailboat) or double-ended.

Double-Ended Sailboat with a
Starboard Sail

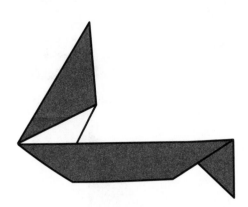

Double-Ended Sailboat with a Raked
Mast and a Full Sail

You can fold the sails in several ways.

Hull shapes, sail and rudder shapes, and stabilizers can all be folded in different combinations to create
unique sailboats. Several folding combinations are shown in the models that follow. This will give you some
ideas about how you want your sailboats to look. The last chapter will explain how to sail your boats. Your
design will determine how the sailboat reacts to the wind. You can also give your sailboat a name. Giving a
sailboat a name is great fun. The first example, "Tabasco," is a play on words. Tabasco is a state in Mexico;
Tabasco peppers and Tabasco sauce are very hot. When a sailboat is "hot," it sails well and is very fast. You
are limited only by your imagination.

Tabasco

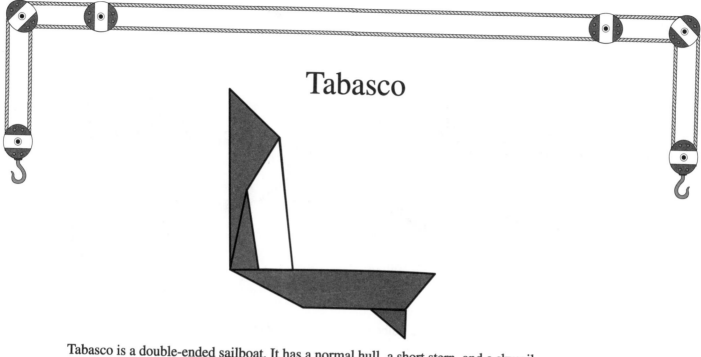

Tabasco is a double-ended sailboat. It has a normal hull, a short stern, and a skysail.

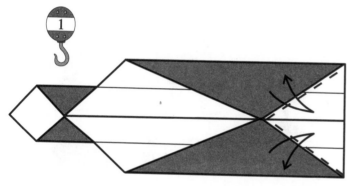

Begin with step 11 of the Short Raked-Stern Sailboat (page 94). Valley-fold the upper and lower right sides of the model along the folded edges and unfold. Make the creases sharp and strong; the shape of the near flaps will be altered during the next few steps.

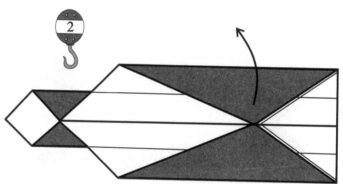

Open the near top flap completely.

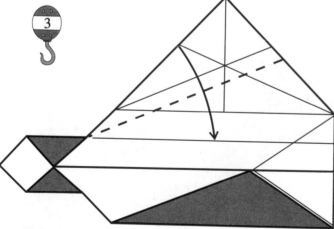

Valley-fold the top left edge down to the first crease as shown.

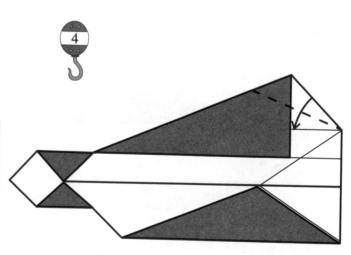

Valley-fold the top right edge down along the existing crease.

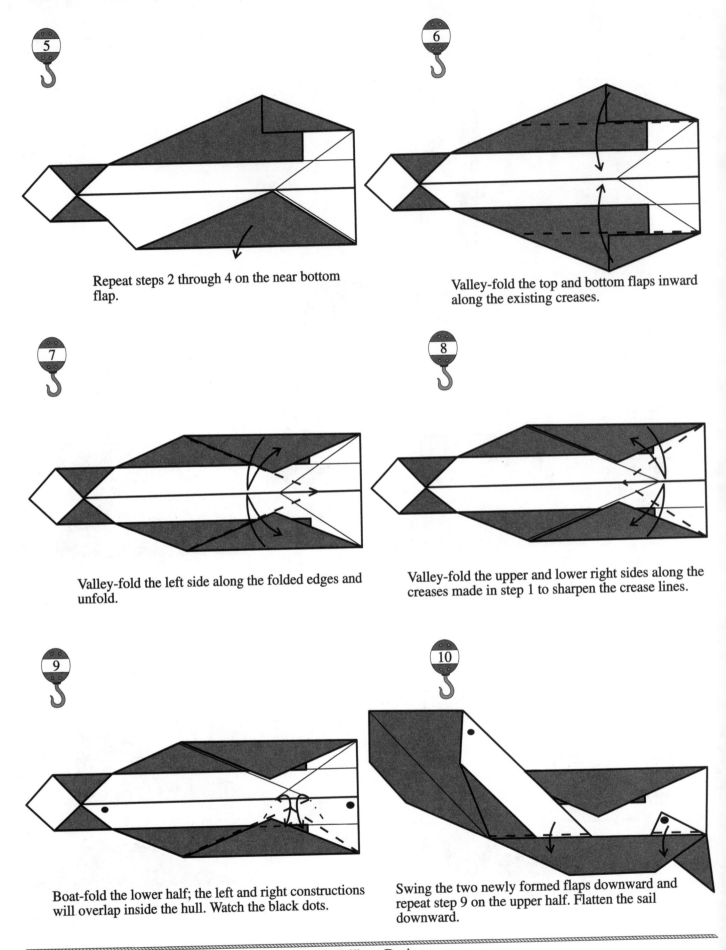

5

Repeat steps 2 through 4 on the near bottom flap.

6

Valley-fold the top and bottom flaps inward along the existing creases.

7

Valley-fold the left side along the folded edges and unfold.

8

Valley-fold the upper and lower right sides along the creases made in step 1 to sharpen the crease lines.

9

Boat-fold the lower half; the left and right constructions will overlap inside the hull. Watch the black dots.

10

Swing the two newly formed flaps downward and repeat step 9 on the upper half. Flatten the sail downward.

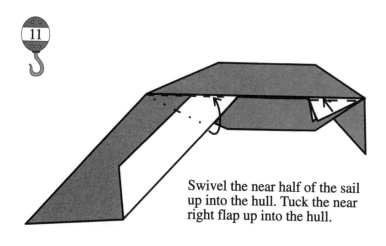

11

Swivel the near half of the sail up into the hull. Tuck the near right flap up into the hull.

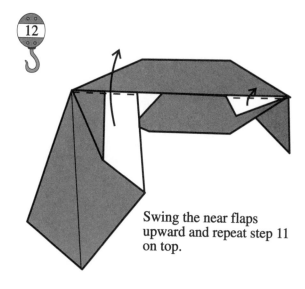

12

Swing the near flaps upward and repeat step 11 on top.

13

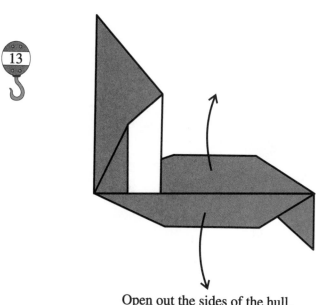

Open out the sides of the hull.

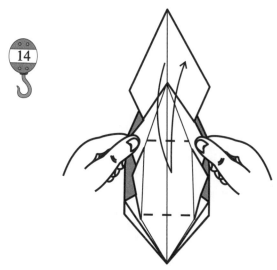

14

Grasp the sides of the hull and valley-fold between the corners and unfold. Repeat at the bottom.

15

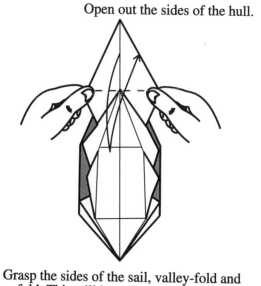

Grasp the sides of the sail, valley-fold and unfold. This will keep the sail open. Adjust the rudder to point downward.

16

The Tabasco Sailboat.

Wind Walker

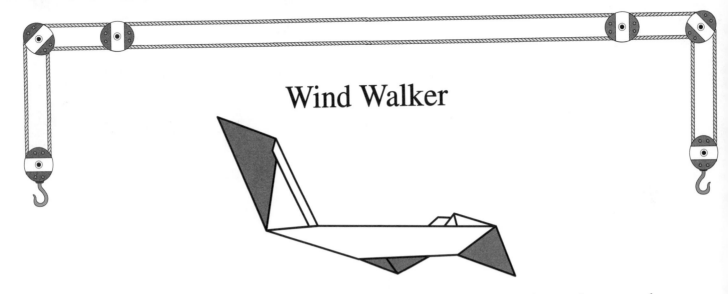

The Wind Walker is a double-ended sailboat. It has a narrow hull, cockpit coamings on the stern, and a long bow. There are two bilge boards and a normal rudder.

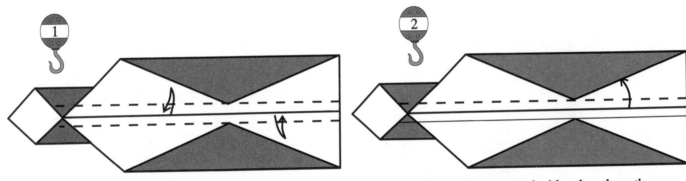

Begin with step 7 of the Double-Ended Sailboat (page 39). Valley-fold the upper and lower halves parallel to the centerline at the points of the near flaps and unfold.

Valley-fold the upper inside edge along the crease formed in step 1 and tuck this edge under the near flap.

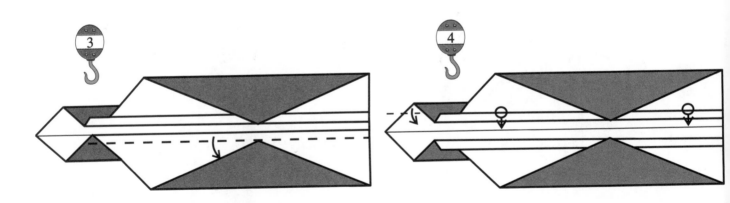

Repeat step 2 on the lower half.

Grasp at the circles the folded cuff of the upper flap and slide the entire flap downward so that its lower edge lies along the centerline. Flatten the model.

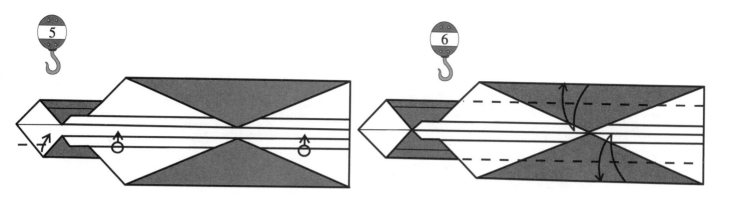

Repeat step 4 on the lower half.

Valley-fold the upper edge down to the centerline and unfold. Repeat below.

Now begin folding the bow and stern of the sailboat. The Wind Walker will have a long bow with a normal stern. Use the folding method for the Double-Ended Long Raked-Bow Sailboat (page 91).

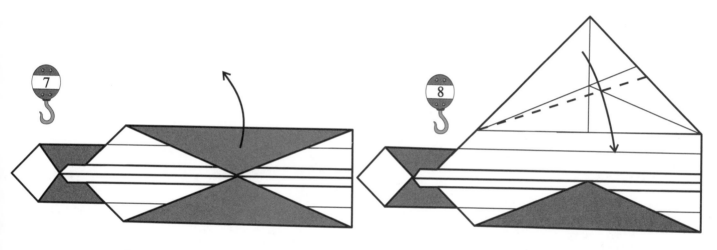

Open the near top flap completely.

Valley-fold the upper left edge down so that its tip touches the horizontal crease made in step 6.

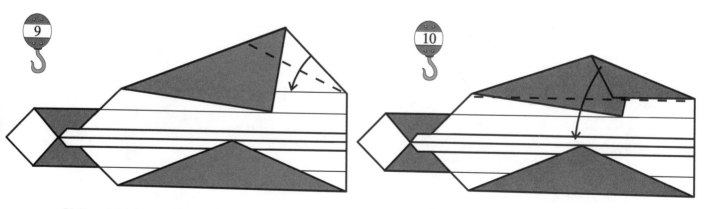

Valley-fold the top flap down along the existing crease.

Valley-fold the top flap downward; the crease is horizontal.

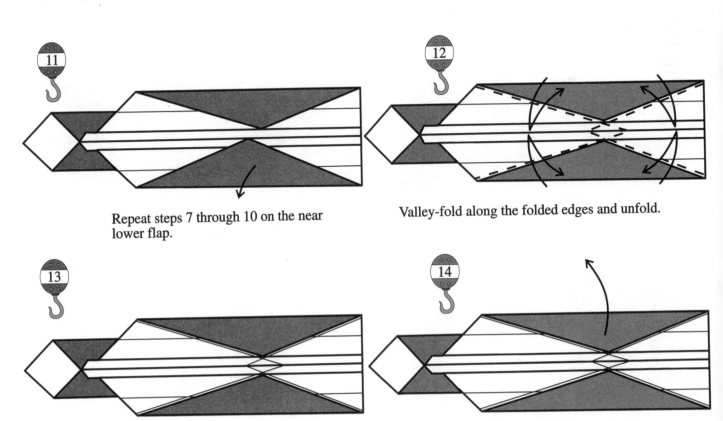

Repeat steps 7 through 10 on the near lower flap.

Valley-fold along the folded edges and unfold.

Before you proceed to the next step be sure that the creases shown in step 13 are strong and sharp.

Open the near top flap completely.

So far you have folded a narrow hull and a long bow. The creases formed in step 12 will be used during the final steps. When you add stabilizers to your models you will not have the edges of the near flaps as guides for folding. You must crease the folds in step 12 very hard. Since the Wind Walker has bilge boards, the near flaps must be folded next.

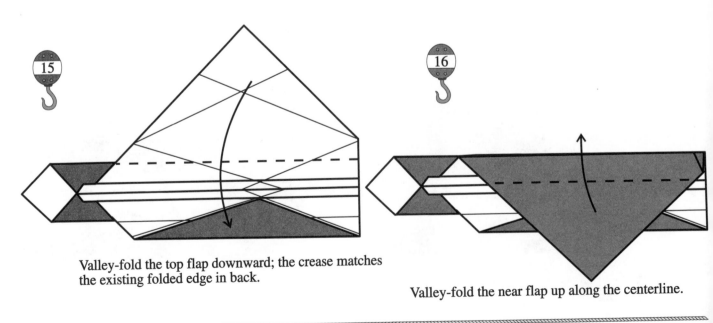

Valley-fold the top flap downward; the crease matches the existing folded edge in back.

Valley-fold the near flap up along the centerline.

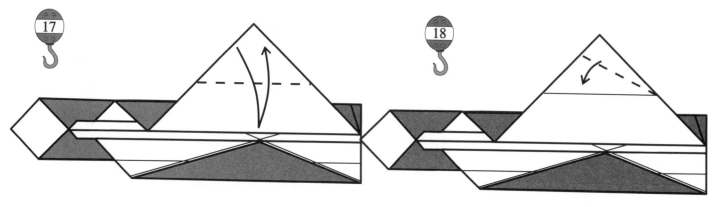

17

Valley-fold the top point down to the crease that
aligns with the rear folded edge and unfold.

18

Valley-fold the top right edge down to the
crease formed in step 17.

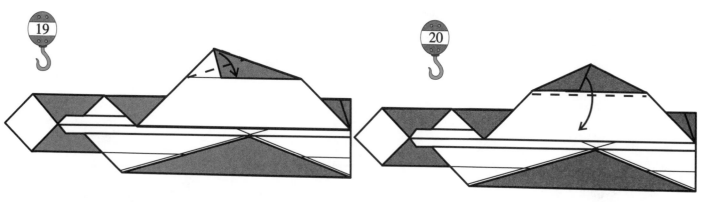

19

Valley-fold the near left edge down to the crease
formed in step 17.

20

Valley-fold the near top flap down along the
crease formed in step 17.

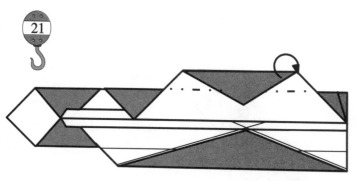

21

Mountain-fold the top near flap back over the single
folded edge just behind it—the flap will lie in the
back groove.

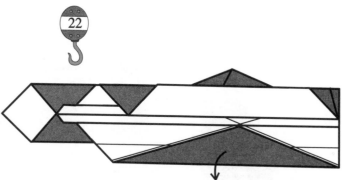

22

Open the bottom near flap completely.
Repeat steps 15 through 21 on the bottom
flap.

The Wind Walker is now ready to be folded into a sailboat. The cockpit coamings will be formed during the final steps. The boat folds will be completed using the existing creases.

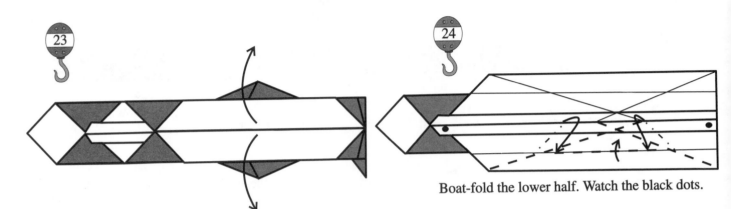

Swing the two near flaps outward in a hinge action.

Boat-fold the lower half. Watch the black dots.

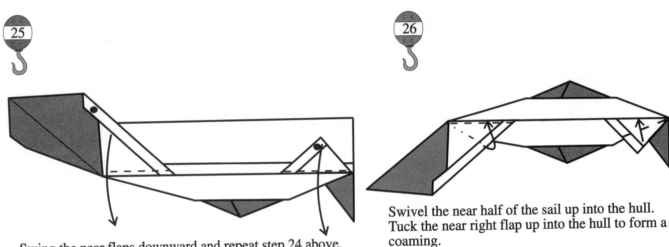

Swing the near flaps downward and repeat step 24 above. Flatten the sail downward.

Swivel the near half of the sail up into the hull. Tuck the near right flap up into the hull to form a coaming.

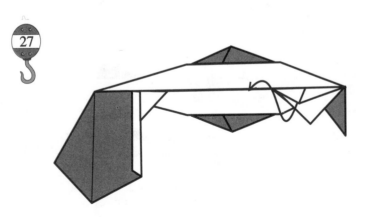

Tuck the near right flap, still pointed downward, down into the hull.

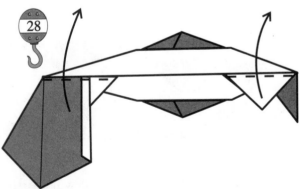

Swing the sail upward and repeat the action of step 26. Swing the small triangular flap upward. Flatten the sail downward.

29

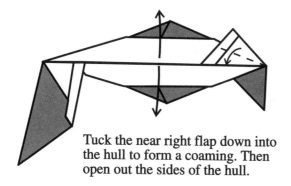

Tuck the near right flap down into the hull to form a coaming. Then open out the sides of the hull.

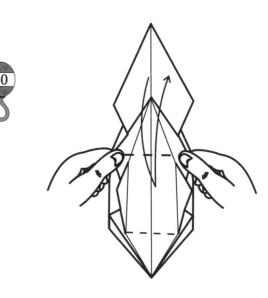

30

Grasp the sides of the hull and valley-fold between the corners and unfold. Repeat at the bottom.

31

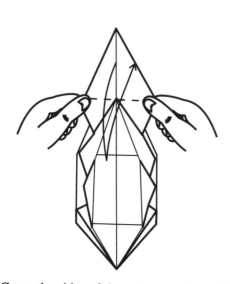

Grasp the sides of the sail and valley-fold and unfold. This will keep the sail open. Adjust the rudder to point downward.

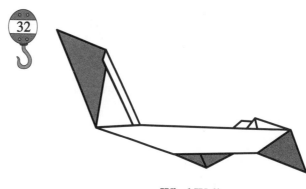

32

Wind Walker

You can fold the Wind Walker with different rudders:

You can fold the sail at different angles:

You can fold the Wind Walker with different stabilizers:

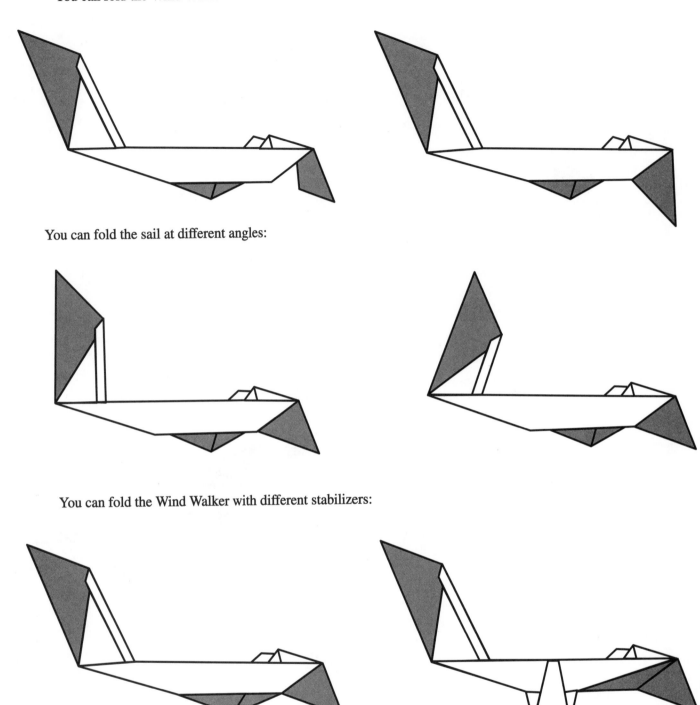

The Tabasco and the Wind Walker are only two sailboat designs out of several hundred you can fold. Choose various elements from previous boats when you design your own sailboat, using the same types of selection as were demonstrated in the Wind Walker.

Sailing Origami Sailboats

Sailing Your Origami Sailboats

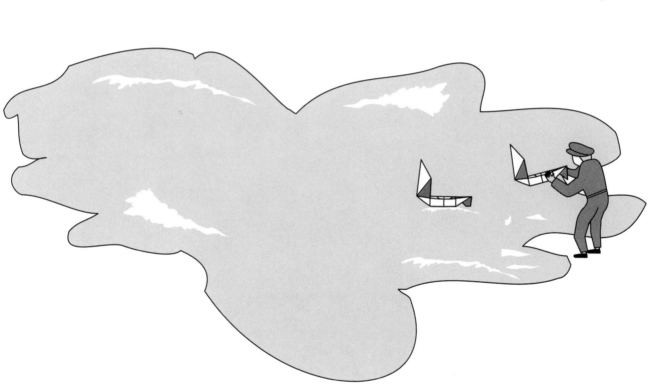

After you have folded your sailboat you will want to sail it. Remember always to keep the wind at your back. The origami sailboats have fixed rudders that do not allow the boats to change course; simply place your sailboat on the water and the wind will do the rest. You can sail your models in a small tub or a large pond or lake. Always sail with a buddy if you choose to sail your model in a large body of water, just to be safe. Remember to take your paper model out of the water when you are finished to protect the environment.

Origami Sailboats in Full Sail

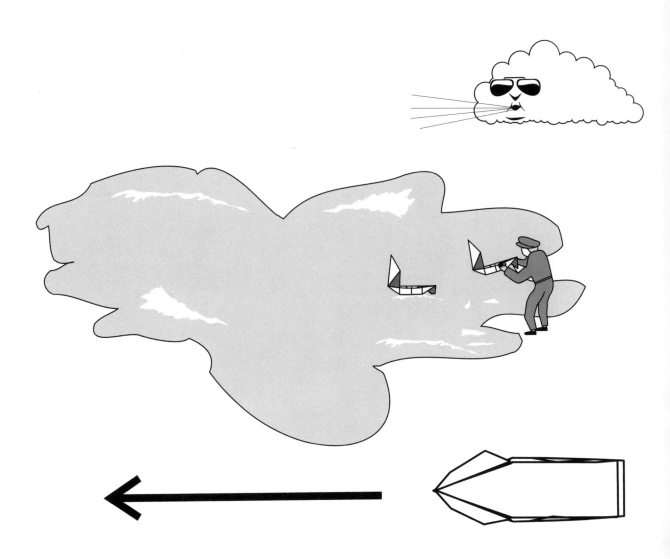

Origami sailboat folded to run dead with the wind in full sail.

When you fold the sailboat with a full sail, it will sail in a straight line with the wind blowing from behind (abaft).

Origami Sailboats in Starboard Sail

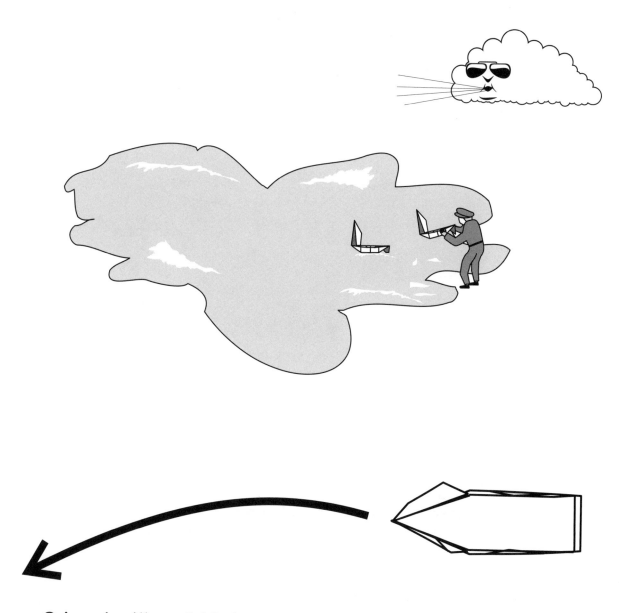

Origami sailboat folded to run in starboard sail.

When you fold the sail with a starboard sail, the boat will sail in a curved line with the wind blowing from behind (abaft). The sailboat will travel in a wide arc to the left (port).

Origami Sailboats in Port Sail

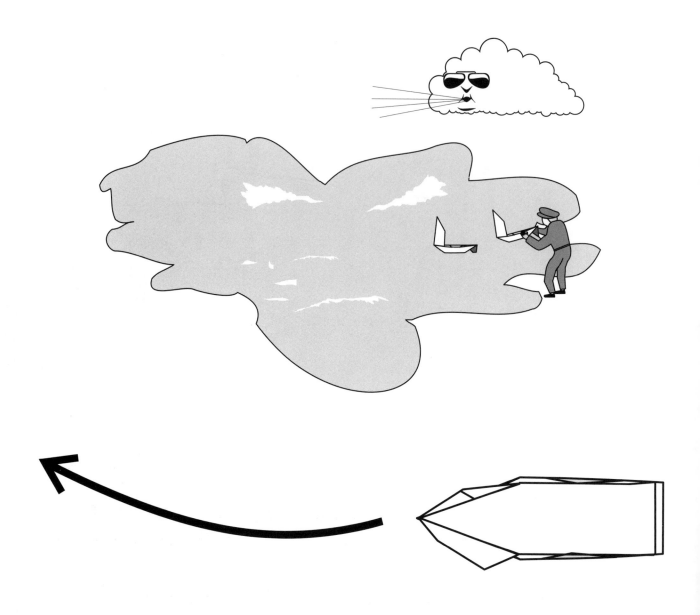

Origami sailboat folded to run in port sail.

When you fold the sail with a port sail, the boat will sail in a curved line with the wind blowing from behind (abaft). The sailboat will travel in a wide arc to the right (starboard).

Origami Sailboats in Half Sail

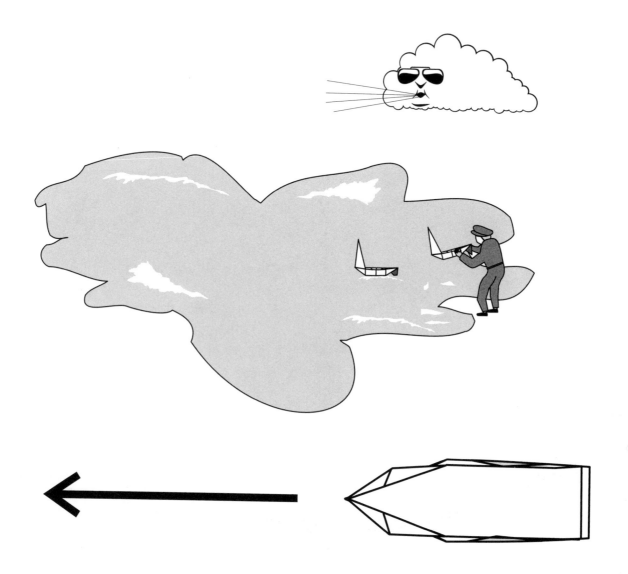

Origami sailboat folded to run dead with the wind in half sail.

When you fold the sail with a half sail, the boat will sail in a straight line with the wind blowing from behind (abaft). The sailboat will travel slowly in a straight line.

Origami Sailboat Regatta

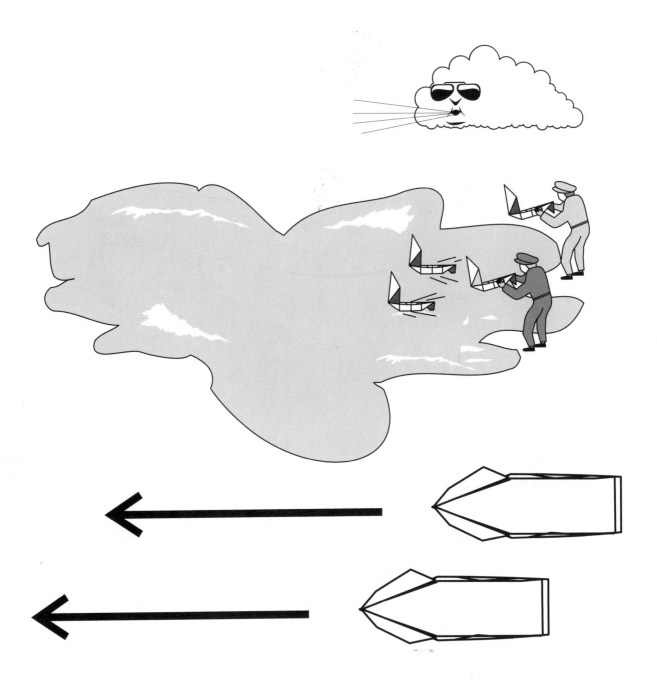

Origami sailboats can be folded in different variations and raced.

Origami sailboats can be raced with a friend's boats, raced against each other, or raced against time with the aid of a watch. Try folding different sailboats and have your own race (regatta).